ARCHAEOLINGUA

Edited by
ERZSÉBET JEREM and WOLFGANG MEID

Series Minor
24

To my mentor, Eugen Kessler

ERIKA GÁL

FOWLING IN LOWLANDS

Neolithic and Chalcolithic Bird Exploitation
in South-East Romania and the Great Hungarian Plain

BUDAPEST 2007

This study was supported by the Hungarian Scientific Research Fund P050163

Front Illustration:
"Leave me alone!"
Grey herons photographed by Dorottya Géczy

Back Cover Illustration:
Prehistoric bird bone remains
Photo by the Author

ISBN 978-963-8046-85-7

HU-ISSN 1216-6847

© ARCHAEOLINGUA Foundation

All rights reserved. No part of this publication may be reproduced, stored in a retrieval system, or transmitted in any form or by any means, electronic, mechanical, digitised, photocopying, recording or otherwise without the prior permission of the publisher.

2007

ARCHAEOLINGUA ALAPÍTVÁNY
H-1250 Budapest, Úri u. 49

Copyediting by Réka Benczes
Desktop editing and layout by Rita Kovács

Printed by Prime Rate Kft

Contents

Foreword 7

1. Introduction 11

2. Geographical and Ecological Background 15
   2.1 South-East Romania 15
   2.2 The Great Hungarian Plain 19

3. Bird Remains from Neolithic Sites in South-East Romania 23
   3.1 Starčevo-Criş culture sites 23
   3.2 Boian-Bolintineanu culture sites 23
   3.3 Boian-Giuleşti culture sites 25
   3.4 Discussion 26

4. Bird Remains from Chalcolithic Sites in South-East Romania 29
   4.1 Gumelniţa A_2 culture sites 29
   4.2 Gumelniţa B_1 culture sites 39
   4.3 Cernavoda I culture sites 40
   4.4 Discussion 40

5. Bird Remains from Neolithic Sites in the Great Hungarian Plain 49
   5.1 Körös culture sites 49
   5.2 Alföld Linear Pottery culture sites 56
   5.3 Bükk–Szilmeg culture sites 57
   5.4 Tisza culture sites 57
   5.5 Herpály–Csőszhalom culture sites 58
   5.6 Discussion 58

6. Bird Remains from Chalcolithic Sites in Hungary 67
  6.1 Tiszapolgár culture sites 67
  6.2 Sites of the Tiszapolgár–Bodrogkeresztúr transition period 67
  6.3 Hunyadihalom culture sites 68
  6.4 Discussion 68

7. Taphonomic Observations on the Assemblages and Individual Remains 73
  7.1 Depositional features 74
  7.2 Modifications on individual bones 75
  7.3 The anatomical distribution of bones 80
  7.4 Discussion 83

8. Pathological Lesions 91

9. Ornithological Implications 93

10. Conclusions 99

References 105

Appendices 123
  Appendix 1. The classification of identified species 123
  Appendix 2. Measurements of avian remains 129

Foreword

The idea for this book was drafted during the study of abundant bird bone assemblages recently excavated from a number of prehistoric archaeological sites in South-East Romania and the Great Hungarian Plain. Although some of the results have already been published in various articles in the past years, this volume summarises the latest results and all the available data. Its aim is to share the information on avian finds and the identified species with archaeologists and archaeozoologists interested in the exploitation of Neolithic and Copper Age environments in the regions discussed. In addition to the specialists involved in the study of bird remains from archaeological assemblages and the history of fowling, this work will also be beneficial for ornithologists by offering information on the species that had once lived or occurred seasonally on the territory of present-day Romania and Hungary.

My studies of subfossil avian remains date back to the mid-1990s when, as a student in biology at the Babeş-Bolyai University in Cluj, I became involved with interdisciplinary projects run by the National Museum of History in Romania. The investigations of bird bones from archaeological samples continued a few years later when I was employed by the Archaeological Institute of the Hungarian Academy of Sciences in Budapest. The parallel studies on the contemporary remains originating from the joint excavations of this institute with Cardiff University, Eötvös Loránd University and several museums in Hungary, as well as from excavations in Romania, gave rise to the idea of synthesising the results in the form of this book.

This volume is dedicated to my mentor, Eugen Kessler, who introduced me to the osteology, as well as to the palaeontology and archaeology of birds. The book is intended to be an acknowledgement of his continuous support, help and advice during the last thirteen years.

This work could not have been completed, however, without the conscientious work of several archaeologists who showed interest in the zoological identification and interpretation of the bird remains they excavated. Among my colleagues in Romania, I wish to thank Radian-Romus Andreescu, Constantin Haită and Dragomir Popovici (National Museum of History in Romania); Douglass Bailey (University of Cardiff); Bernard Randoin (Ministry of Culture and Communication, France); Silvia Marinescu-Bîlcu (Archaeological Institute of Bucharest); Stănica Pandrea (Museum of Brăila); Marian Neagu (Museum of the Lower Danube); Cătălin Borțun, Cristi Mirea, Ion Pătrașcu, Mirea Pavel and Pompilia Zaharia

(Museum of Teleorman County); Gheorghe Matei (Museum of Ialomița); Elena Renţa (OPCN Ialomița); and Cristian Micu (Museum of Tulcea) for inviting me to work on the excavated avian bones. My fellow archaeozoologists, Adrian Bălăşescu, Dragoş Moise and Valentin Radu, are especially acknowledged for selecting the bird bones for study and for the archaeological information they have provided.

For the bones excavated in Hungary, I am grateful to János Makkay and István Zalai-Gaál (Archaeological Institute of the Hungarian Academy of Sciences); Alasdair Whittle (University of Cardiff); Dénes Jankovich-Bésán (National Office of Cultural Heritage); Pál Raczky (Institute of Archeological Sciences of the Eötvös Loránd University); Piroska Csengeri, Judit Koós and Róbert Patay (Herman Ottó Museum, Miskolc); László Domboróczki (Dobó István Museum, Eger); and János Dani (Déri Museum, Debrecen). I also wish to thank my fellow archaeozoologists, László Bartosiewicz, Márta Daróczi-Szabó and István Vörös, for providing additional bird bones for the purposes of analysis.

I am especially indebted to László Bartosiewicz for having revised the manuscript from both an archaeozoological and a linguistic point of view. His suggestions greatly improved the quality of this work.

I am grateful to Erzsébet Jerem, Managing Director of the Archaeolingua Foundation and Publishing House, for supporting the idea of this publication. The final English text was kindly revised by Réka Benczes. András Kardos, Rita Kovács and Fruzsina Cseh provided graphical and editorial help.

The identification of the majority of bird remains presented in this work was made possible by study trips to reference collections in Europe. These visiting fellowships were granted by the European Committee – Research Infrastructure activity in the framework of the 5th (COBICE 2002, COLPARSYST 2004) and 6th (DK-TAF 2005, AT-TAF 2005) Programmes. My hosts, Kim Aaris-Sørensen and Anne Birgitte Gottfredsen (Zoological Museum, University of Copenhagen); Christine Lefèvre (Laboratory of Comparative Anatomy, National Museum of Natural History, Paris); and Ernst Bauernfeind (Bird Collection, Museum of Natural History, Vienna) kindly provided access to the bird bone collections and local infrastructure.

I would also like to thank Mihály Gasparik and Piroska Pazonyi for allowing me to access the bird bone collection of the Museum of Natural History in Hungary. My work in Hungary was supported by the Domus Hungarica Scientiarum et Artium Junior Fellowship (2000, 2001) and the Bolyai János Fellowship (2005–2008) within the framework of the Hungarian Academy of Sciences, as well as by the project F 048818 (2005–2008) of the Hungarian Scientific Research Found (OTKA). An earlier part of my research was completed during a fellowship granted by the Romanian Government in 2002.

Finally, special thanks go to my family who supported me throughout my research and tolerated all those weekends and holidays that I spent on studying bones and staying in front of the computer.

1. Introduction

Archaeo-ornithology is a special field within archaeozoology. Bird remains are usually under-represented in archaeological samples excavated in Central and Eastern Europe. This observation holds especially for bone assemblages accumulated during prehistoric periods, when only wild birds were available.

The scarcity of avian samples can be explained by a number of reasons, partly rooted in the distant past, and partly accountable by present-day factors. The low economic value of birds in comparison with mammals, as well as the intense mobility and seasonal presence of a rather great number of avian species, made their hunting more difficult and rarely worthwhile for ancient peoples.

Birds differ from mammals in their osteological characteristics as well. During evolution, the avian skeleton of birds modified in accordance with their special way of life, that is, flying. These changes include both quantitative and qualitative ones. The reduction in the number of bones in the skeleton and the fragility of skeletal parts increase the possibility of taphonomic loss of these usually small finds. Thus the application of proper methods of recovery during archaeological excavations is essential in reliably retrieving bird bones. Incomparably more avian remains were recovered from sites where the excavated soil was water-sieved or dry-screened, as opposed to those settlements where animal bones were collected only by hand.

Since the number of bird species living in a certain habitat tends to be relatively high and the remains of closely related avian taxa are often found in excavated samples, the identification of bones from wild fowl requires the use of comparative collections. The small number of well-supplied reference collections and specialists trained in the identification of bird bones also contributed to the remarkable scarcity of archaeo-ornithological studies (GÁL 2006a).

Although a great number of archaeological excavations targeted Neolithic and Copper Age settlements in Hungary, only a few bird remains are known from the majority of these sites. Since they were often selected from rather abundant archaeozoological materials (BÖKÖNYI 1974), we may assume that the main reason for the characteristically small size of avian assemblages is the hand collection of bones. Additionally, the lack of bird bone specialists fully devoted to archaeo-ornithological studies resulted in the fact that, with a few exceptions (BÖKÖNYI 1992a), the remains were published in catalogue-like review articles (BÖKÖNYI – JÁNOSSY 1965; JÁNOSSY 1985). The situation was similar in Romania, where incomparably fewer avian remains were studied and published from archaeological samples (JURCSÁK – KESSLER 1986; JURCSÁK – KESSLER 1988).

Multidisciplinary studies that emerged along with intensive archaeological excavations carried out in South-East Romania since the 1990s have completely changed this picture. A relatively great number of avian bones have been recorded as a result of sieving during these field campaigns and the careful selection of bird remains (GÁL – KESSLER 2002; GÁL – KESSLER 2003). The application of modern methods of recovery gave rise to more abundant bird bone assemblages in Hungary as well (GÁL 2007a; GÁL 2007b; RACZKY et al. 2007).

This trend became especially important from the viewpoint of understanding the way of life of people, since bones seem to be the only reliable evidence when studying prehistoric fowling methods and the targeted species. Egg shells are especially fragile remains, whose chances of recovery are minimal compared to that of bones. Even when a few remains are discovered, such as those from the Hârşova tell (RADU 2003a: 191, Fig. 111), restoring the egg shell from small fragments is almost impossible, and the identification of egg remains requires special techniques and expertise (SIDELL 1993).

In spite of the lack of egg shell finds from prehistoric settlements in Hungary, ethnological and etymological analogies show that the gathering and utilization of eggs and feathers – complementing fishing, and gathering pond tortoise (*Emys orbicularis* Linnaeus, 1758) as well as leech (*Hirudo medicinalis* Linnaeus, 1758) – were important ancient subsistence activities in the marshy environment of the Great Hungarian Plain. The eggs of grebes, swans, geese, ducks, galliforms and crows seemed to have been collected most commonly even in the 20th century (GUNDA 1979: 15–27).

The role of archaeological artefacts that could have been used in birding is uncertain and most probably multiple. From the viewpoint of the methods of hunting and gathering, fowling does not seem to be as specialised an activity as fishing. While a rather great number and variety of fishing gear such as antler harpoons and net-weights are known from both the region of the Lower Danube and the Great Hungarian Plain (e.g. BANNER 1940; KOREK 1958; VOINEA 1997; SCHUSTER 2002), no special archaeological evidence points to the killing of birds. Nevertheless, nets, largely used in fishing, as well as nooses and bolas, could have also been applied in the trapping and hunting of birds (GOTFREDSEN – MØBJERG 2004: 137, Fig. 152).

Otherwise, hunting methods in fowling were most probably closer to methods used in the hunting of mammals. Lances and bows must have been the most frequently used weapons. Evidence from the Early Middle Ages (LIGETI 1962) and North Eurasian ethnographic sources indicate that blunt-tipped arrows were used in fowling, since these did not damage the skin or the plumage of birds. Some of these arrows were even made from long bird bones (KODOLÁNYI 1976, Fig. 5), thereby taking advantage of the lightness of avian skeletal parts.

In addition, the simple hitting of birds, especially the terrestrial species, whose females and juveniles stay in the nest, could have been an even simpler way of killing. The scapula of Bewick's swan, showing a healed trauma (Chapter 8, Plate 3), can be considered as evidence for such intervention. It is worth mentioning, however, that swans are rather watchful birds, usually staying in the middle of water surfaces, and thus difficult to approach (PÁK 1829: 122). The hunting of moulted and numbed great bustards and cranes in chilly mornings, when birds were unable to take flight, was an efficient method in the Great Hungarian Plain as late as the 20th century (ORTUTAY 1977: 555–556).

Consequently, the identification of avian bones from archaeological samples seems to be the only consistent method for acquiring systematic information on prehistoric fowling. This synthesis presents all the archaeo-ornithological data available from the Neolithic and Chalcolithic of South-East Romania and the Great Hungarian Plain studied to date. The sites are listed proceeding from east to west (starting with Romania) in a chronological sequence, and alphabetically within archaeological periods. *Tables 1* and *2* summarise the sites and periods presented in both countries. From a taphonomic point of view, it is essential to know the methods of archaeological recovery applied at each site, since these determine the number of recovered bone remains, and consequently, the number of recognized species. The use or lack of water-sieving or dry screening has a direct impact on the size and composition of avifaunal assemblages. Thus *Tables 1* and *2* include information regarding this issue as well.

The color maps illustrate the location and topographic situation of sites. Since this work is an evaluation of bird remains, I have provided only a brief description of sites. Publications on the non-avian bone remains, as well as general information concerning the archaeozoological results in the examined regions and periods, are also provided in the discussions closing each chapter.

When enumerating the species identified in the text, I gave only the English names of birds in order to save space. The taxonomic status of the discussed species is provided in Appendix 1. The classification of birds used in my work follows the traditional morphological, rather than the DNA-based, taxonomy. Since a number of works on nomenclature had appeared that resulted in inconsistencies in the literature, the author and year of description are not provided here above the level of species. Those regarding species have been used as listed by CRAMP (1998). Both the Latin and English names of birds are to be found in the summarizing tables arranged by countries and archaeological periods, in order to make the species lists easily comprehensible for non-English speakers and native English-speakers alike.

These tables also include the number of identifiable specimens (NISP) per taxa and site, and show the minimum number of individuals (MNI) calculated by skeletal part, body side, age and sex. Abbreviations indicating habitat preferences are as follows: A – aquatic, S – steppe, W – woodland, FS – forest-steppe, GF – gallery forest, MT – mountainous, U – ubiquist. Abbreviations indicating the seasonal presence of species: R – resident, SV – summer visitor, WV – winter visitor, P – passage, V – vagrant. Bold print indicates the seasonal presence of species, as developed in recent centuries. Abbreviations indicating the feeding behaviour of birds are: H – herbivorous, C – carnivorous, I – insectivorous, S – scavenger, O – omnivorous. Most of the data concerning the distribution and characteristics of species were taken from CRAMP's (1998) general work. Nevertheless, information concerning the seasonal presence, breeding sites and other – "region-specific" – data were collected from a number of ornithological works completed in the countries studied.

The degree of fragmentation was described using three different terms in *Tables 5–6* and *10–11*. In addition to "complete", the word "incomplete" was used to denote slightly damaged specimens, whose measurements could not be taken in every dimension. The term "fragment" was reserved for bird bones that retained only one of the epiphyses or were preserved in even smaller pieces.

Appendix 2 includes the measurements of complete and fragmentary bones on which at least one epiphysis was found intact. The measurements, taken by a digital calliper to a precision of 0.1 mm, follow the international standard developed by Angela VON DEN DRIESCH (1976).

2. Geographical and Ecological Background

2.1 South-East Romania

South-East Romania is located near the Black Sea, bordering on the modern-day territories of Ukraine, Moldova and Bulgaria. Covering approximately 45,000 km², it includes three main geographical regions: the Romanian Lowland, the Plateau of Dobrogea and the Danube Delta (*Fig. 1*). The Romanian Lowland, the largest relief unit in the country, is bordered by the marshy pastures of the Danube from the west, south and east. The Danube, together with its branches, the Borcea and the Old Danube, form two large, frequently inundated valleys in the east: Balta Ialomiței and Balta Brăilei. The Getic Plateau, the Sub-Carpathians and the Plateau of Moldova form the northern boundary of the Romanian Lowland.

The Romanian Lowland lies on Mezozoic and Neozoic rocks. The Pliocene and Quaternary layers of gravel, clay, sand and loess (up to 40 m in thickness) filled up the basin of the Pontic Lake that was once located here from north to south and west to east. This is also the direction in which the lowland slopes, determining the direction of streams. The surface is very much divided by the valleys and marshlands formed by a number of larger and smaller rivers, such as the Danube, the Olt and the Jiu, as well as the Călmățui, the Teleorman, the Arges, the Ialomița, etc. The altitude of the Romanian Lowland ranges from 6 m to 300 m, but is at an average of 50–90 m in most of the region.

Dobrogea is located between the Danube and the Black Sea. Its surface, including the Danube Delta – which in turn, does not belong to Dobrogea from a physical-geographical point of view – is approximately 15,485 km². The relief is not as uniform as that of the Romanian Lowland. The Măcinului Hills, mostly formed by old granite, are found in Northern Dobrogea. Their highest peak is 467 m. The Plateaus of Babadag, Casmicei and Dorobanțului lie south of this hilly region, and their altitudes vary between 200–325 m. Both the northern and central parts of Dobrogea slope west to east, from the direction of the Danube to the Black Sea.

South Dobrogea is located on more recently formed rocks (limestone and sandstone) and its altitude is below 200 m. This part of the region has an inverse sloping direction from the sea toward the Danube, and is covered by loess in large areas. Aside from the marshy floodplain of the Danube and its delta, Dobrogea is essentially a steppe, interrupted by several wooded areas in the north and the south.

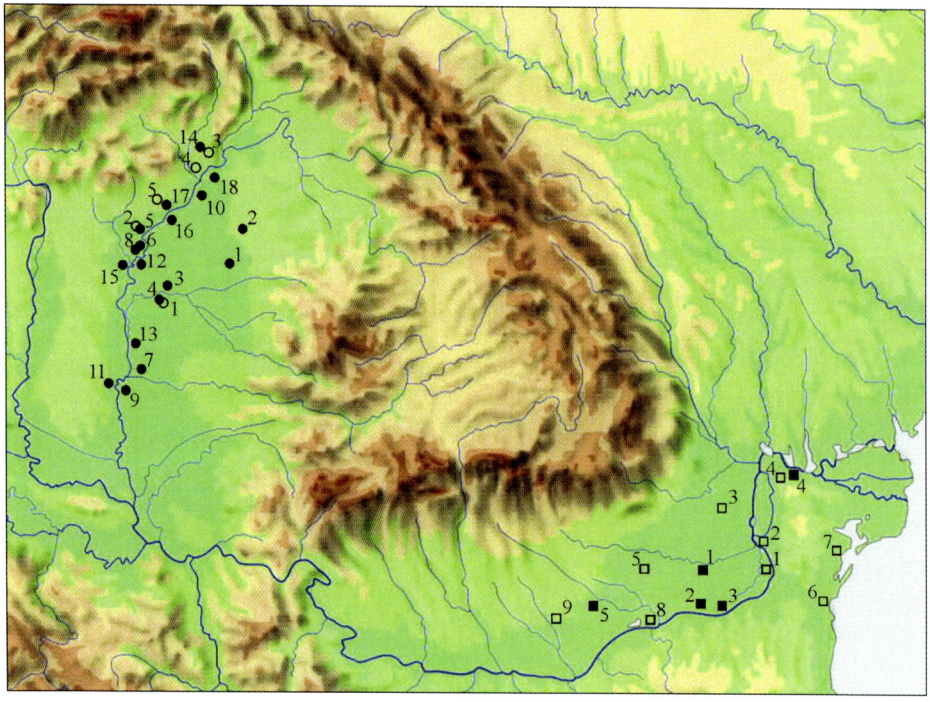

Fig. 1. The location of sites that yielded avian finds in South-East Romania and the Great Hungarian Plain (base map by L. Zentai).

Neolithic sites in Romania (full squares):
1. Ciulniţa; 2. Gălăţui; 3. Grădiştea–Coslogeni; 4. Isaccea–Suhat;
5. Măgura–Buduiasca.

Chalcolithic sites in Romania (empty squares):
1. Borduşani–Popină tell; 2. Hârşova tell; 3. Însurăţei–Popina I tell;
4. Luncaviţa–Cetăţuie tell; 5. Măriuţa tell; 6. Năvodari–La Ostrov–Taşaul tell;
7. Panduru tell; 8. Căscioarele tell; 9. Vităneşti tell.

Neolithic sites in Hungary (full circles):
1. Berettyószentmárton; 2. Debrecen–Nyulas; 3. Ecsegfalva 23;
4. Endrőd 6, Endrőd 39 and Endrőd 119; 5. Kisköre–Gát; 6. Kőtelek–Huszársarok;
7. Maroslele–Pana; 8. Nagykörű–Tsz.; 9. Őszentiván (Tiszasziget);
10. Polgár–Folyás and Polgár–Csőszhalom; 11. Röszke–Lúdvár;
12. Szajol–Felsőföld; 13. Szegvár–Tűzköves; 14. Szerencs–Taktaföldvár;
15. Szolnok–Szanda; 16. Tiszaszőlős–Domaháza; 17. Tiszavalk–Négyesi-határ;
18. Tiszavasvári–Keresztfal.

Chalcolithic sites in Hungary (empty circles):
1. Kisköre–Szingegát; 2. Mezőzombor–Községi temető; 3. Tiszalúc–Sarkad;
4. Tiszavalk–Tetes.

From a climatic point of view, South-East Romania is the warmest (annual average temperature above 11°C, with -3 to 0°C in January and above 23°C in July) in the marshland of the Danube, along the coast of the Black Sea and in the Danube Delta. A mean annual temperature of 10–11°C (-6 to -3°C in January and 20–23°C in July) is characteristic of the main part of the Romanian Lowland, as well as the Plateau of Dobrogea, excluding the hilly regions, where the average annual temperature falls to 6–10°C. The smallest amount of precipitation falls in the eastern and northern parts of the Romanian Lowland (400–500 mm/year) as well as in Dobrogea and the Danube Delta (less than 400 mm/year). Most of the rain (500 to 700 mm/year) falls in the main part of the lowland. Droughts are rather characteristic of this region. Even these present-day data show the main differences within the region. From a palaeo-climatic point of view, the Neolithic and Chalcolithic belong to the Atlantic stage. This period, lasting from 5500 to 2250 BC, was the climatic optimum in the Holocene, characterized by a warm and humid climate.

The vegetation belongs to three main formations both in the Romanian Lowland and Dobrogea. The natural vegetation of the plain has been replaced by crop cultivation in most of its area. Marshlands with willows (*Salix*) and poplars (*Populus*) are mostly characteristic along the valleys of the Danube, the Siret and the Ialomița rivers. Steppe grassland is found in the eastern area. The forest-steppe is formed by grasses (Poacea) and oak trees (*Quercus*), which maintain the region's characteristic fauna.

The vegetation in Dobrogea has an ancient character; its actual age is dated to approximately 3,000 years. The steppe, typical of the southern region below 100 m altitude, is of the largest expansion. The forest-steppe is mostly characteristic of the western and south-western areas. Among the trees, oak, hornbeam (*Carpinus*) and ash (*Fraxinus*) are worth mentioning. Forests are underrepresented in modern-day Dobrogea. They are mostly found in the mountains where linden (*Tilia*), oak and hornbeam are the most frequent species.

The majority of the studied Neolithic and Chalcolithic settlements are located in the eastern (10 sites) and northern (2 sites) part of the Romanian Lowland. Most of them were found along the Danube or other rivers. Only the tell settlements of Năvodari–La Ostrov–Tașaul and Panduru are located in the littoral zone of the Plateau of Dobrogea.

Neolithization arrived to the present-day territory of Romania during the 7th millennium BC by successive migrations of peoples from Anatolia. The Neolithic was characterized by the presence of ceramics since its beginning dated to approximately 6,100 calBC. It includes the following cultures in South-East

Table 1. The chronological sequence and methods of recovery used at Romanian sites.

Age	Culture	Phase	Site	Methods of recovery
Chalcolithic	Cernavoda	I	Hârşova tell	Hand-collected and wet-sieved
Chalcolithic	Gumelniţa	B1	Vităneşti tell	Hand-collected
Chalcolithic	Gumelniţa	B1	Măriuţa tell	Most probably hand-collected only
Chalcolithic	Gumelniţa	B1	Căscioarele tell	Most probably hand-collected only
Chalcolithic	Gumelniţa	A2	Panduru tell	Most probably hand-collected only
Chalcolithic	Gumelniţa	A2	Năvodari–Taşaul–La Ostrov tell	Hand collected and wet-sieved
Chalcolithic	Gumelniţa	A2	Luncaviţa–Cetăţuie tell	Hand-collected and wet-sieved
Chalcolithic	Gumelniţa	A2	Însurăţei–Popina I tell	Hand-collected
Chalcolithic	Gumelniţa	A2	Hârşova tell	Hand-collected and wet-sieved
Chalcolithic	Gumelniţa	A2	Borduşani–Popină tell	Hand-collected and wet-sieved
Neolithic	Boian	Giuleşti	Isaccea–Suhat	Hand-collected and wet-sieved
Neolithic	Boian	Giuleşti	Ciulniţa	Hand-collected
Neolithic	Boian	Bolintineanu	Grădiştea–Coslogeni	Wet-sieved
Neolithic	Boian	Bolintineanu	Gălăţui–Movila Berzei	Most probably hand-collected only
Neolithic	Dudeşti			
Neolithic	Starčevo-Criş		Măgura–Buduiasca	Hand-collected and wet-sieved

Romania: Starčevo-Criş (Early Neolithic), Dudeşti and Boian (Middle Neolithic) and Hamangia (Late Neolithic). The Boian culture has been divided into four phases, namely Bolintineanu, Giuleşti, Vidra and Spanţov. The Gumelniţa culture marks the beginning of the Chalcolithic in this region at approximately 4,000 calBC. It has been divided into three stages: Gumelniţa A_1, Gumelniţa A_2 and Gumelniţa B_1. The best known culture in the Middle Chalcolithic is Cernavoda I, while Cernavoda III and Coţofeni mark the Late Chalcolithic (approximately 2,750 calBC; MANTU 1995: 223–224, Fig. 2). The avian material under study represented the Starčevo-

Criş, Dudeşti, Boian-Bolintineanu and Boian-Giuleşti cultures within the Neolithic, and Gumelniţa A_2 and Gumelniţa B_1 within the Chalcolithic (*Table 1*).

2.2 The Great Hungarian Plain

The Great Hungarian Plain, the second largest lowland in Europe, is the largest geographical unit in modern-day Hungary. The region that occupies over half of the country is bordered by the North Hungarian Mountains, the North-Eastern Carpathians, the Mountains of Bihar in the east and the Dinaric Alps in the south. A part of the Great Hungarian Plain extends over the Danube, thus its western borders are formed by the Transdanubian Mountains and the Transdanubian Hills. Its total extension is approximately 100,000 km², of which approximately 50,000 km² lies within the present borders of Hungary. The Great Hungarian Plain extends to the territories of modern-day Slovakia, Ukraine, Romania and Serbia. Three main regions constitute it within the confines of Hungary: Mezőföld on the right bank of the Danube, the territory of the Danube–Tisza Interfluve, and the Hungarian territory east of the Tisza.

The Great Hungarian Plain was covered by the Pannonian Sea during the Tertiary, approximately between 12–5.4 My BP (hence the synonym Pannonian Plain). Its recent geology is characterized by tertiary layers in the marginal regions, as well as Quaternary and Holocene sediments (gravel, sand, loess and mud) in its largest part. The redeposition of shifting sand became especially characteristic during the Holocene. Primary dolomite settled on sand or loess layers formed in the alkaline lakes of the Plain. In the northeast, the peat bog of Ecsed developed.

The altitude of the Great Hungarian Plain ranges between 78–183 m, the average altitude being approximately 120 m in the eastern and 80 m in the southern region. The beds of numerous rivers and their branches cut into the thick – sometimes more than 70 m deep – loess. The Danube, the largest river, divides Hungary into two regions by flowing in a north to south direction through the central part of the country. Today the Tisza, the second largest river, meanders across the Great Hungarian Plain towards the east along a more than 600 km long course. It was shortened by 453 km in the second part of the 19th century, when 136 major bends (!) were cut. The main tributaries of the Tisza are the following: the Bodrog and the Sajó with the Hernád and the Zagyva (on the right bank), and the Túr, the Szamos, the Kraszna, the Körös and the Maros (on the left bank). These rivers often changed their courses during the Holocene, leaving numerous oxbows behind. The complex system of rivers and channels has formed a varied, mosaic-like environment in both the ancient and the present-day flood plains (SÜMEGI *et al.* 2003).

The climate of the Great Hungarian Plain is variable and extreme. The annual average temperature is 10.4°C, with mean temperatures of -1.6°C in January and 21.5°C in July. Changes of 10–15°C within a day are not unusual in this region. Droughts and inundations are equally characteristic. The annual precipitation varies between 400–900 mm, the average being 600 mm.

The Great Hungarian Plain falls into the zone of forest-steppe in its entirety (i.e. beyond the political borders of Hungary). Originally it was a loess and sand-covered region interspersed by marshlands and gallery-forests. Owing to recent river regulations and tillage, however, its largest part became a cropland, and the loess and sand plains, marshlands and forest-steppe survive only in small, island-like areas. The vegetation consists of species characteristic of the eastern plains of Europe. Needlegrass (*Stipa*), reed (*Phragmites*) and saline plants are especially common. Altogether there are about 20 indigenous plant species living in the marshlands and the sand and loess plains of this region.

The overwhelming majority of the Neolithic and Copper Age sites that yielded the avian remains under discussion in this work are located along the Tisza and its tributaries over a rather large territory (*Fig. 1*). The temperate and humid climate of the long Atlantic period was warmer by 2–3°C than the modern-day average temperature. Oak forests, as well as gallery forests, formed by willows and poplars along the rivers and marshlands, were frequent during this period in the Great Hungarian Plain.

Considering the soil, the climate and the hydrography, it has been suggested that Neolithization in the Carpathian Basin took place along the river valleys that represented so-called "green corridors". However, a largely south-west to north-east diagonal line – the Central European-Balkan Agroecological Barrier (CEB AEB; SÜMEGI *et al.* 2002) – has been determined by environmental archaeological studies across the Carpathian Basin, which apparently limited the northward distribution of the Körös-Starčevo culture of south-eastern origins, thereby slowing down the spread of agriculture. Most sites from the Great Hungarian Plain under discussion fall south of this line.

The Neolithic period begins with the Körös culture in the Great Hungarian Plain, which marks the Early Neolithic around 6,000 BC. The Middle Neolithic includes the Alföld Linear Pottery culture (ALPC), as well as the Szatmár II and Bükk cultures. The Neolithic ends at around 4,200 BC with the Szakálhát, Tisza and Herpály cultures. As it is suggested by the diversity of ceramic styles, a relatively great number of cultures had developed during the approximately 1,500 years of the Copper Age in the Great Hungarian Plain. While only the Proto-Tiszapolgár and Tiszapolgár cultures mark the Early Copper Age in this region, the Bodrogkeresztúr and the Hunyadihalom cultures are characteristic of the Middle Copper Age. The Late Copper Age includes the Proto-Boleráz, Boleráz and Baden cultures (BÁNFFY 1997: 61). Most of the cultures from both the Neolithic and Chalcolithic are represented by the avian material under discussion (*Table 2*).

Table 2. The chronological sequence and methods of recovery used at Hungarian sites.

Age	Culture	Site	Methods of recovery
Chalcolithic	Hunyadihalom	Tiszalúc–Sarkad	Hand-collected
	Tiszapolgár-Bodrogkeresztúr	Tiszavalk–Tetes	Hand-collected
	Tiszapolgár	Mezőzombor–Temető	Hand-collected
		Kisköre–Szingegát	Hand-collected
Neolithic	Herpály-Csőszhalom	Polgár–Csőszhalom	Hand-collected
		Berettyószentmárton–Herpály	Hand-collected
	Tisza	Szerencs–Taktaföldvár	Hand-collected
		Szegvár–Tűzköves	Hand-collected
		Kisköre–Gát	Hand-collected
	Bükk-Szilmeg	Polgár–Folyás	Hand-collected
	Alföld Linear Pottery	Tiszavasvári–Keresztfal	Hand-collected
		Tiszavalk–Négyesi határ	Hand-collected
		Kőtelek–Huszársarok	Hand-collected
		Endrőd 6	Hand-collected
		Debrecen–Nyulas	Hand-collected
	Körös	Tiszaszőlős–Domaháza–Puszta–Réti-dűlő	Hand-collected
		Szolnok–Szanda	Hand-collected
		Szajol–Felsőföld	Hand-collected
		Röszke–Lúdvár	Hand-collected
		Ószentiván (Tiszasziget)	Hand-collected
		Nagykörű–Tsz.	Hand-collected
		Maroslele–Pana	Hand-collected
		Kőtelek–Huszársarok	Hand-collected
		Endrőd 119	Hand-collected
		Endrőd 39	Hand-collected
		Ecsegfalva 23	Wet-sieved and dry-screened

3. Bird Remains from Neolithic Sites in South-East Romania

3.1 Starčevo-Criş culture sites

Măgura–Buduiasca (Teleorman County)

The site is located on the lower terrace of the Teleorman river (*Fig. 1*), at about 10 km northeast from the city of Alexandria. It has been under excavation since 2001 within the framework of the South Romanian Archaeological Project (SRAP), directed by Radian Andreescu, Cristi Mirea and Douglas Bailey. The settlement shows traces of the Neolithic Starčevo-Criş, Dudeşti and Vădastra cultures. Radiocarbon data place the Starčevo-Criş habitation to around 5700 BC (CIMEC 2004a). The non-avian archaeozoological material was studied by Adrian Bălăşescu (BĂLĂŞESCU 2003a: 43–44).

Eleven bird remains were found in Starčevo-Criş culture features during the 2003 field season. Six specimens could be identified to the species level, including the great bustard, the tawny eagle and the rook/hooded crow (*Table 3*). The single bone from a tawny owl was found in Complex 1, while the rest of the remains from Starčevo-Criş features originate from the closed Complex 13. According to the sizes of the skeletal parts, the bones from the great bustard belonged to a female. Four unidentifiable bones originate from large birds, while one comes from a medium-size bird. One bone that was identified as belonging to a white-tailed eagle was brought to light from Complex 25. This feature contained artefacts of the Dudeşti culture, showing Karanovo III stylistic elements. In this section an anthropomorphic bust has also come to light (CIMEC 2004a).

3.2 Boian-Bolintineanu culture sites

Gălăţui–Movila Berzei (Călăraşi County)

The site is located on the upper terrace of the southern shore of Lake Gălăţui, between the localities of Alexandru Odobescu and Gălăţui. The rescue excavations were directed by Marian Neagu during the early 1980s (CIMEC 2001). The non-avian archaeozoological material was studied by Adrian Bălăşescu (BĂLĂŞESCU 2003a). Only a single avian find was found in 1984, assigned to a female great bustard (*Table 3*).

Table 3. List of bird taxa identified from Neolithic sites in South-East Romania (NISP/MNI).

Taxon		Habitat	Seasonality	Food	Starčevo–Criș	Dudești	Boian–Bolintineanu		Boian–Giulești	
					Măgura–Buduiasca		Gălățui–Movila Berzei	Grădiștea–Coslogeni	Ciulnița	Isaccea–Suhat
Podiceps cristatus	Great crested grebe	A	SV	C						1
Pelecanus onocrotalus	White pelican	A	SV	C						1
Egretta alba	Great white egret	A	SV/R	C						4/1
Ardea purpurea	Purple heron	A	SV	C				1		
Ciconia cf. ciconia	White stork	FS	SV	C					1	
Cygnus olor	Mute swan	A	SV/R	H					1	5/1
Anser anser	Grey-lag goose	S	SV/R	H					2/1	1
Anas penelope	Wigeon	A	P/WV	O				1		
Anas platyrhynchos	Mallard	A	R	O				1	1	
Anas sp.	unidentifiable duck	A	?	O				1		
Pernis apivorus	Honey buzzard	FS	SV	I						
Haliaeetus albicilla	White-tailed eagle	GF	R	C		1				
Accipiter gentilis	Goshawk	W	R	C					1	
Aquila chrysaetos	Golden eagle	W	R	C/S						1
Tetrao tetrix	Black grouse	FS	R	O				2/1	1	
Grus grus	Crane	S	SV	C				1		
Otis tarda	Great bustard	S	R	C	3/1		1		1	
Columba palumbus	Woodpigeon	W	SV/R	H	1			1		
Strix aluco	Tawny owl	W	R	C	1					
Corvus frugilegus/C. corone	Rook/Carrion crow	FS	R	O						1
Aves indet.	unidentified bird	?	?	?	6			1	2	1
Total					12/4	1	1	10/8	10/7	15/7

Grădiştea–Coslogeni (Călăraşi County)

Grădiştea–Coslogeni is located in the Danube Valley, in Balta Borcei, a flood plain area between the Danube and one of its branches, the Borcea. The excavations were directed by Marian Neagu in 1997–1998 (CIMEC 2000a). The non-avian archaeozoological material was studied by Adrian Bălăşescu and Valentin Radu (BĂLĂŞESCU 2003a; RADU 2001a). Ten bird bones were found that belonged to at least eight birds. The species that were identified included the following: purple heron, wigeon, mallard, honey buzzard, black grouse, crane and woodpigeon (*Table 3*). Four remains of a purple heron, a black grouse and a woodpigeon, respectively, were excavated from feature C2Gr1, a pit that held the traces from phase II of the Hamangia culture (CIMEC 1997a).

3.3 Boian-Giuleşti culture sites

Ciulniţa (Ialomiţa County)

The site is located on the terrace of the Ialomiţa river. Rescue excavations were carried out in 1994–1995 under the direction of Silvia Marinescu-Bîlcu, Gheorghe Matei and Elena Renţa (CIMEC 1994). The non-avian archaeozoological material was studied by Adrian Bălăşescu and Valentin Radu (BĂLĂŞESCU 2003a; RADU 2000a; 2003a). Only ten remains of at least seven birds were found. The identified species are as follows: white stork, mute swan, grey-lag goose, mallard, goshawk, black grouse and great bustard (*Table 3*). Two unidentifiable bones originate from large birds. According to the bone sizes, the hawk was a female, while the black grouse was a male.

Isaccea–Suhat (Tulcea County)

Isaccea is located north of the Măcin Mountains and the Plateau of Dobrogea, on the right bank of the Danube. Excavations at this site in 1997–1998 were directed by Cristian Micu (MICU et al. 2000). The non-avian archaeozoological material was studied by Adrian Bălăşescu and Valentin Radu (BĂLĂŞESCU 2003a; RADU 2000c). A total of fifteen bird bones have been excavated, representing at least seven individuals. The species identified are as follows: great crested grebe, white pelican, great white egret, mute swan, gray-lag goose, golden eagle and rook/hooded crow (*Table 3*). The distal fragment of tibiotarsus from a white pelican originates from a subadult bird.

3.4 Discussion

Both non-avian and bird remains are modestly represented at the South-East Romanian Neolithic sites discussed above. Although the settlements at Grădiştea–Coslogeni and Isaccea yielded considerable numbers of fish bone (RADU 2003a: 288, 293) and the number of mammalian material remains from Ciulniţa also stands out from among the others (BĂLĂŞESCU 2003a: 69–76), these assemblages fall behind the Chalcolithic deposits in terms of size.

Only five sites yielded skeletal parts of birds. Măgura–Buduiasca, the Starčevo-Criş culture habitation is the single settlement that represents the Early Neolithic in this region. The other four sites were inhabited during the Middle- and Late Neolithic. Gălăţui–Movila Berzei and Grădiştea–Coslogeni hold the traces of the Boian–Bolintineanu culture, while Ciulniţa and Isaccea–Suhat represent the next phase of this period by artefacts characteristic of the Boian-Giuleşti culture.

The number of excavated specimens ranges from a single bone to fifteen remains. In the case of these samples the number of recovered avian bones does not reflect unambiguously a close relation to the applied excavation methods. Four of the five sites yielded at least 10 remains, depending on whether a part or all the soil samples were wet screened. Only the Gălăţui–Movila Berzei site, where the remains were simply collected by hand, yielded a single bird bone (*Table 1*, *Table 3*).

The number of birds identified to the level of species is also small. A maximum of eight individuals were recognized from Grădiştea–Coslogeni. A total of 20 avian taxa were identified, 19 of them to the level of species. Most of the birds were identified from the sites of Grădiştea–Coslogeni, Ciulniţa and Isaccea–Suhat: seven species from each. It is worth mentioning, however, that the calculated MNI values indicate only one individual per species at these sites as well (*Table 3*).

The best-represented birds in the Neolithic period of Romania are aquatic fowl. Species living in steppe, forest-steppe and woodland habitats were identified in smaller numbers (three-four species per ecotype). Usually different ecotypes were present at each site. Nevertheless, open wetland species dominate Grădiştea–Coslogeni and Isaccea–Suhat. Fish remains were also abundant at these sites, with thousands of bones and more than 10 identified taxa (RADU 2000c; RADU 2003a). More steppe birds have been identified from Ciulniţa. At the same time, very few fish bones and a small number of species, yet 15 different mammalian species were identified among the over 3000 remains at this site (BĂLĂȘESCU 2003a: 69).

The great bustard has been identified from three different settlements, the rest of the species occurred at two sites at most. These include the mute swan, the graylag goose, the mallard, the black grouse and the rook/crow. Except for the latter, all aforementioned bird species are relatively large and considered to be tasty even today. Diurnal birds of prey were identified at three sites, but with only one species per settlement. The single owl species (tawny owl) was identified from the Măgura–Buduiasca site, where the white-tailed eagle had also been hunted. The song birds are represented by the rook/crow only. It has been described from Măgura–Buduiasca and Isaccea–Suhat. In contrast with the other four sites, the total absence of aquatic species was noted at Măgura–Buduiasca.

Most of the birds identified from the Neolithic deposits are summer visitors and residents in South-East Romania. All four species found at Măgura–Buduiasca are sedentary. The wigeon is the single fowl that is a passage or winter visitor in this area. It was described from the site of Grădiștea–Coslogeni. In addition to the remains of summer visitors, the unossified tibiotarsus from a white pelican offers evidence for seasonal bird hunting at Isaccea–Suhat.

From an economic point of view, it is evident that the provision of meat was based on animal husbandry at Ciulnița, Gălățui–Movila Berzei and Măgura–Buduiasca. Eighty to ninety percent of the identifiable bone specimens derived from domestic species (*Fig. 2*). There was a relatively high proportion of hunted mammals and birds at Măgura–Buduiasca, but this is most probably a random phenomenon, attributable to small assemblage size. On the other hand, fishing complemented by hunting and gathering seems to have been widely practiced at Grădiștea–Coslogeni and Isaccea–Suhat, owing to the proximity of the Danube (*Fig. 1*). Nevertheless, the application of water-sieving during the excavations at these sites also resulted in the recovery of a great number of fish remains (BĂLĂȘESCU – RADU 2002: 78).

Bones of cattle, followed by Caprinae (sheep or goat) and pig yielded the majority of bone remains from domestic animals at most Neolithic sites studied here. The Isaccea–Suhat settlement is an exception, however, since dog was the second most commonly exploited domesticate. Marks of skinning, butchery and burning discovered on the skeletal parts of rather small-sized dogs (mean withers height = 37.35 cm) are indicative of the multiple exploitation of the earliest domesticated animal in the Lower Danube region (BĂLĂȘESCU 2003a; RADU 2003a). At this site, dog bones (87) together with the remains of wild animals

(154) made up 44% of the mammalian remains identifiable to the level of species (RADU 2003a: 293, Table 7). This fact adds new evidence to the observation that the consumption of dogs would have been more characteristic in Neolithic communities, whose economy relied more heavily on hunting (BARTOSIEWICZ 2005: 53–54, Fig. 6.3).

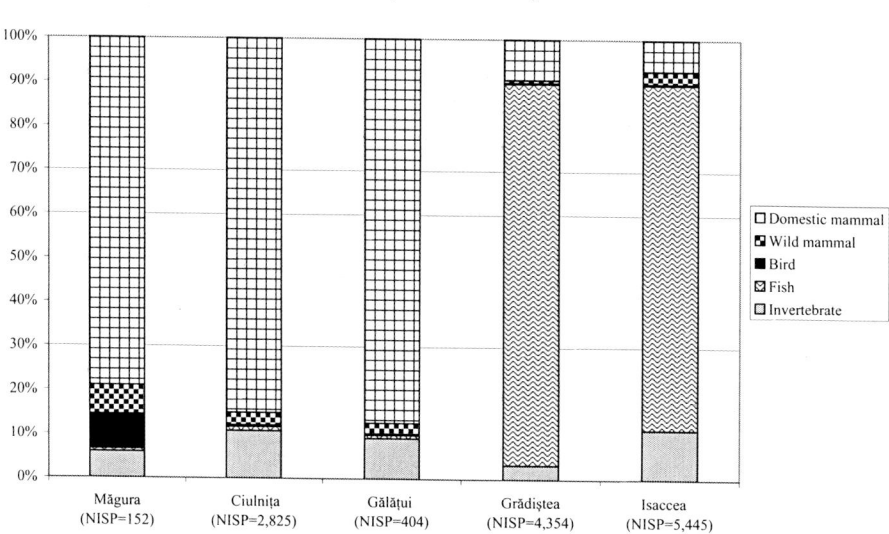

Fig. 2. *Percentual distributions of the number of identifiable specimens (NISP) of the main animal groups at the Neolithic sites in South-East Romania.*

4. Bird Remains from Chalcolithic Sites in South-East Romania

4.1 Gumelniţa A_2 culture sites

Borduşani–Popină tell (Ialomiţa County)

The 15.4 m high, oval-shaped tell site, measuring 180 by 70 m, lies 2.5 km north-east from the village of Borduşani. It is located in the Balta Ialomiţei Plain, surrounded by the Borcea channel of the Danube and the Danube itself (MARINESCU-BÎLCU 1997). Excavations that yielded the bird remains studied here were directed by Silvia Marinescu-Bîlcu and Dragomir Popovici between 1993–2000.

Both the archaeological and archaeozoological results from this settlement have been summarized in two summary works (1997 and 2003). The non-avian animal remains were studied by Adrian Bălăşescu, Valentin Dumitraşcu, Dragoş Moise, Valentin Radu and Márton Venczel (MOISE 1997; RADU 1997; VENCZEL 1997; BĂLĂŞESCU *et al.* 2003; RADU 2003a; RADU 2003b). Following the preliminary report on the 69 avian remains excavated in 1993–1994 (KESSLER – GÁL 1997), a more complete study including taphonomic, palaeoecological, seasonal and biometric observations has recently been published (GÁL – KESSLER 2003).

A total of 287 bird bones were found in the Gumelniţa culture deposits excavated between 1993–2000. Most of them derive from phase A_2 of this culture that represents the interval between 4550–3950 BC (BEM 2001). The avian remains indicated the presence of at least 50 birds from the following species: great crested grebe, cormorant, great white egret, grey heron, black stork/white stork, glossy ibis, mute swan/whooper swan, gray-lag goose, teal, mallard, pintail, garganey, pochard/scaup, ferruginous duck, white-tailed eagle, imperial eagle, booted eagle, black grouse, partridge, coot, crane, great bustard, hoopoe, magpie, rook/hooded crow and raven (*Table 4*). A number of remains were found within houses, building complexes and pits (*Table 5*). Nevertheless, the majority of finds originate from deposits in which the remains of the houses have been discovered.

Table 4. List of bird taxa identified from Chalcolithic sites in South-East Romania (NISP/MNI).

Taxon		Habitat	Seasonality	Food	Gumelnița A2							Gumelnița B1			Cernavoda I
					Bordușani-Popina	Hârșova	Însurăței	Luncavița	Năvodari	Panduru	Vitănești	Căscioarele	Măriuța	Vitănești	Hârșova
Podiceps cristatus	Great crested grebe	A	SV	C	1	1			1						1
Podiceps nigricollis	Black-necked grebe	A	SV	C					1						
Phalacrocorax carbo	Cormorant	GF	SV/R	C	11/1	19/4		2/1	9/2					1	
Pelecanus onocrotalus	White pelican	A	SV	C		2/1	1							1	
Botaurus stellaris	Bittern	A	SV/R	C		3/1									
Nycticorax nycticorax	Night heron	GF	SV	C		1									
Egretta garzetta	Little egret	GF	SV	C		1									
Egretta alba	Great white egret	A	SV/R	C	17/2	2/2						1		1	
Ardea cinerea	Grey heron	GF	SV/R	C	15/3	22/3									
Ardea purpurea	Purple heron	A	SV	C	4/1	9/2									
Ciconia cf. ciconia	White stork	FS	SV	C		5/1									
Ciconia nigra/ C. ciconia	Black stork/ White stork	GF/FS	SV	C	7/?							1			
Plegadis falcinellus	Glossy ibis	GF	SV	C	3/1	3/2									
Ciconiiformes sp. indet.	unidentifiable wading bird				1/(?)	6/?									1
Cygnus olor	Mute swan	A	SV/R	H		3/1	2/1	1	7/1						
Cygnus columbianus	Bewick's swan	A	WV	H		1									
Cygnus cygnus	Whooper swan	A	WV	H		10/3						2/1		5/1	

				Gumelniţa A2							Gumelniţa B1			Cernavoda I
Taxon	Habitat	Seasonality	Food	Bordușani-Popină	Hârșova	Însurăței	Luncavița	Năvodari	Panduru	Vitănești	Căscioarele	Măriuța	Vitănești	Hârșova
Cygnus olor/ C. cygnus	A		H	26/4	30/?									1
Anser fabalis/ A. erythropus	S	P/WV	H		1									
Anser anser	S	SV/R	H	33/4	133/7	1					4/1		1	7/1
Anser sp.								1						
Anas cf. strepera	A	SV/R	O					1						
Anas crecca	A	WV	O	1									1	
Anas platyrhynchos	A	R	O	45/6	2/1	1		1			1		9/3	
Anas acuta	A	R	O	4/1				1						
Anas querquedula	A	SV	O	4/3			1							
Anas sp.				6/?	3/?				1					
Aythya ferina/A. marila	A		O	1									1	
Aythya nyroca	A	SV/R	O	2/2										
Aythya fuligula	A	WV/R	O					1						
Anatidae sp. indet.	A		O	1									2/?	
Pernis apivorus	FS	SV	I		1									
Haliaeetus albicilla	GF	R	C		9/1						1			
Gypaetus barbatus	MT/FS	R	C/S										1	
Circus macrourus	S	SV	C										1	
Accipiter gentilis	W	R	C		2/1									

31

Taxon		Habitat	Seasonality	Food	Bordușani–Popină	Gumelnița A2						Gumelnița B1			Cernavoda I
						Hârșova	Însurăței	Luncavița	Năvodari	Panduru	Vitănești	Căscioarele	Măriuța	Vitănești	Hârșova
Buteo buteo	Buzzard	FS	R	C		2/2									
Aquila pomarina	Lesser spotted eagle	GF	SV	C		1						1			
Aquila cf. clanga	Spotted eagle	GF	SV	C		1									
Aquila heliaca	Imperial eagle	FS	SV/R	C	1										
Aquila chrysaetos	Golden eagle	W	R	C/S		2/1									
Aquila sp.	unidentifiable eagle					1									
Hieraaetus pennatus	Booted eagle	W	SV	C		1						1			
Pandion haliaetus	Osprey	GF	SV/P	C		1									
Accipitriformes sp. indet.	unidentifiable diurnal bird of prey					3/?									
Falco cf. peregrinus	Peregrine	U	R/WV	C											
Tetrao tetrix	Black grouse	FS	R	H	3/1						2/1			22/3	
Perdix perdix	Partridge	S	R	H/I	2/2	1								1	
Porzana porzana	Spotted crake	A	SV	C		1									
Gallinula chloropus	Moorhen	GF	SV	C		3/1									
Fulica atra	Coot	A	SV/R	C	12/3	1			2/1						
Grus grus	Crane	S	SV	C	1			1	1		1	1		6/1	
Anthropoides virgo	Demoiselle crane	S	SV/P	C										1	
Tetrax tetrax	Little bustard	S	R/P	C	1									1	
Otis tarda	Great bustard	S	R	C							1	2/1	1	20/3	
Columba palumbus	Woodpigeon	W	SV/R	H		3/1					1			1	
Strix aluco	Tawny owl	W	R	C										1	
Asio flammeus	Short-eared owl	S	R	C										1	
Upupa epops	Hoopoe	FS	SV	I	2/1										

Taxon		Habitat	Seasonality	Food	Gumelnița A2							Gumelnița B1			Cernavoda I
					Bordușani-Popină	Hârșova	Însurăței	Luncavița	Năvodari	Panduru	Vitănești	Căscioarele	Măriuța	Vitănești	Hârșova
Riparia riparia	Sand martin	S	SV	I		5/1									
Hirundo rustica	Barn swallow	S	SV	I		12/2									
Turdus pilaris	Fieldfare	FS	WV/R	I										1	
Pica pica	Magpie	FS	R	O	3/1	7/1									
Corvus frugilegus/ C. corone	Rook/Carrion crow	FS	R	O	20/4	19/4								3/1	
Corvus corax	Raven	RF	R	O	1										
Passeriformes sp. indet.						24/?									
Aves indet.	unidentifiable bird				52/?	90/?	2/?		5/?		2/?			15/?	5/?
Total					287/50	448/58	10/6	6/5	33/14	1	6/4	16/11	1	97/27	15/4

Table 5. List of species and skeletal parts identified from dwellings (SL), house complexes (C) and pits at the Borduşani Popină tell.

Feature	US	Species	Bone	Side	Fragmentation	Note
SL 12	1598	*Ciconia nigra/C. ciconia*	ulna	sin	fragment	
SL 43	3724	*Plegadis falcinellus*	ulna	sin	fragment	
			radius	sin	fragment	
			carpometacarpus	sin	incomplete	
SL 43 A6	3724	*Anas platyrhynchos*	radius		fragment	
	3724	*Corvus frugilegus/C. corone*	ulna	sin	fragment	
C 46		*Egretta alba*	cranium		complete	
			mandibula		incomplete	
			vertebra (9)		complete	
			femur	dex	incomplete	
			tibiotarsus	sin	incomplete	
			tibiotarsus	dex	incomplete	
			tarsometatarsus	sin	complete	
			tarsometatarsus	dex	complete	
C 143	2525	*Ardea cinerea*	carpometacarpus	sin	incomplete	
	2525	*Ardea purpurea*	humerus	sin	fragment	
	2525		carpometacarpus	sin	complete	
	2525	Ardeiformes sp. indet.	mandibula		fragment	
		Anas platyrhynchos	carpometacarpus	sin	complete	
	2525	*Anas sp.*	humerus	sin	fragment	juvenile
	2525	*Perdix perdix*	ulna	dex	complete	juvenile
	2525	*Fulica atra*	radius	sin	fragment	
	2529	*Fulica atra*	tarsometatarsus	dex	fragment	
	2525	*Fulica atra*	tarsometatarsus	sin	fragment	
	2525	*Corvus frugilegus/C. corone*	scapula	dex	fragment	
	2525	Aves indet.			fragment	gnawn
	2525	Aves indet.			fragment	
C 160		*Anser anser*	sternum		fragment	
		Anser anser	radius	sin	fragment	
C 186		*Phalacrocorax carbo*	ulna	dex	fragment	
C 194	2820	*Ardea cinerea*	ulna	dex	fragment	
C 195		*Ardea cinerea*	carpometacarpus	sin	fragment	
C 201	2808	*Ardea cinerea*	ulna	dex	fragment	
	2808	Aves indet.	humerus		fragment	
C 230	3960	*Ciconia nigra/C. ciconia*	ulna	sin	fragment	

Feature	US	Species	Bone	Side	Fragmentation	Note
C 234	4174	*Phalacrocorax carbo*	humerus		fragment	
C 277	4166	*Phalacrocorax carbo*	carpometacarpus	dex	complete	
	4166	*Anas platyrhynchos*	ulna	dex	complete	
	4166	*Hieraaetus pennatus*	carpometacarpus	dex	complete	
	4166	*Corvus frugilegus/C. corone*	ulna	sin	fragment	
pit (trench C5)		*Ardea cinerea*	tibiotarsus	dex	fragment	
		Anas plaryrhynchos	coracoideum	dex	complete	
			carpometacarpus	sin	complete	
		Fulica atra	humerus	dex	fragment	
	1070	*Fulica atra*	ulna	sin	fragment	
		Corvus frugilegus/C. corone	scapula	sin	incomplete	
			humerus	sin	incomplete	
			radius	sin	fragment	
			tibiotarsus	dex	fragment	
			tibiotarsus	dex	incomplete	
			tibiotarsus	dex	fragment	
		Pica pica	tarsometatarsus	sin	complete	
		Aves indet.	sternum		fragment	
			sternum		fragment	
			sternum		fragment	
pit (trench J4)		*Anas platyrhynchos*	coracoideum	sin	complete	
			coracoideum	dex	fragment	
			scapula	sin	fragment	
			scapula	dex	fragment	
			humerus	sin	complete	
			humerus	dex	complete	
			ulna	sin	complete	
			ulna	dex	complete	
			radius	dex	complete	
			carpometacarpus	sin	complete	
			femur	sin	fragment	
			femur	dex	complete	
			tibiotarsus	sin	complete	
			tibiotarsus	dex	complete	
			tarsometatarsus	sin	complete	
			tarsometatarsus	dex	complete	
		Pica pica	humerus	sin	complete	
pit (trench B2C)		*Anser anser*	humerus	dex	fragment	

Hârşova tell (Constanţa County)

This site, located on the right bank of the Danube, falls within the boundary of the city of Hârşova. The 12 m high, 200 m long and 150 m wide Neolithic tell settlement has been under continuous excavation for almost two decades, which has resulted in the richest Chalcolithic avian material from South-East Romania. Since 1993, excavations directed by Dragomir Popovici have continued within the framework of a bilateral project between the Romanian and French cultural ministries (POPOVICI *et al.* 2000). The non-avian animal bones were studied by Nathalie Desse-Berset, Dragoş Moise and Valentin Radu (DESSE-BERSET – RADU 1996; MOISE 2000; RADU 2000b; RADU 2003a).

No avian remains were found in the Neolithic levels of this settlement. The layers containing Gumelniţa culture (phase A_2) finds made up approximately 7 m of the stratigraphy at this tell site. This section yielded the majority of the avian material, while a small number of remains were recovered from the younger, Cernavoda I culture features (HAŞOTTI – POPOVICI 1992). Preliminary results on 225 bird bones have recently been published (GÁL – KESSLER 2002).

Herewith all 448 remains known so far are presented. They can be assigned to at least 57 individuals representing the following 36 species: great crested grebe, cormorant, white pelican, bittern, night heron, little egret, great white egret, grey heron, purple heron, white stork, glossy ibis, mute swan, Bewick's swan, whooper swan, bean goose/lesser white-fronted goose, gray-lag goose, mallard, honey buzzard, white-tailed eagle, goshawk, buzzard, lesser spotted eagle, imperial eagle, golden eagle, booted eagle, osprey, partridge, spotted crake, moorhen, coot, little bustard, woodpigeon, sand martin, barn swallow, magpie and rook/hooded crow (*Table 4*). As with the Borduşani–Popină tell, a number of remains were found in house complexes (*Table 6*).

Însurăţei–Popina I tell (Brăila County)

The site is located in the Călmăţui Valley, on the right bank of the river, approximately 6 km north of the city of Însurăţei. The tell is 11 m high and 250 m long (CIMEC 1995). Ten avian bones were brought to light from Gumelniţa A2 culture features during the field season directed by Stănică Pandrea in 1998. The non-avian animal bones were studied by Dragoş Moise and Valentin Radu (MOISE 1999; RADU 1999; RADU 2003). The majority of bird remains were found in dwellings. The six bird species identified include the white pelican (Dwelling 4), the mute swan (Dwelling 1), the gray-lag goose (Dwelling 1), the mallard (Dwelling 1), the white-tailed eagle and the black grouse (Dwelling 6) (*Table 4*).

Table 6. List of species and skeletal parts identified from house complexes (C) at the Hârşova tell.

Feature	US	Species	Skeletal part	Side	Fragmentation	Note
C 13	1129	Anser anser	radius		fragment	subadultus
C 330	3549	Cygnus cygnus/C. olor	coracoideum	dex	fragment	
C 436	4130	Anser anser	vertebra		complete	
			ulna		fragment	
			carpometacarpus		fragment	
C 448	3641	Anser anser	humerus	dex	fragment	
C 458	3659	Anser anser	radius	sin	complete	
C 509	3813	Anser anser	carpometacarpus	dex	complete	
C 521	5392	Egretta alba	tibiotarsus	dex	fragment	
	4423	Ardea cinerea	coracoideum	dex	fragment	
	4309		humerus	dex	fragment	
	5116		humerus	sin	fragment	
	5356		radius	dex	fragment	
	5039		tibiotarsus	dex	fragment	
	5356	Ardea purpurea	humerus	sin	fragment	
	5423		radius	sin	fragment	
	5356	Plegadis falcinellus	coracoideum	sin	fragment	
	5392		coracoideum	sin	incomplete	
	5374		tibiotarsus	sin	fragment	
	5149	Ardeiformes sp. indet.	tibiotarsus		fragment	subadultus
	4338	Anser anser	ulna	dex	fragment	
	5009		ulna	dex	fragment	
	5101		ulna		fragment	
	5031		femur	dex	fragment	
	5109		tibiotarsus	dex	fragment	
	5140		tarsometatarsus	dex	fragment	
	4436	Anas sp.	humerus	dex	fragment	
	5356	Buteo buteo	carpometacarpus	sin	incomplete	male
	4489	Accipitriformes sp. indet.	phalanga pedis (toe)		complete	
	5123		phalanga pedis		fragment	
	4482	Porzana porzana	tibiotarsus	dex	fragment	
	5009	Gallinula chloropus	scapula	sin	fragment	
	5009		humerus	sin	fragment	
	5009		ulna	sin	complete	
	5071	Corvus frugilegus/C. corone	humerus	dex	fragment	
	5231		radius	dex	fragment	
	4213		tibiotarsus	sin	fragment	

Feature	US	Species	Skeletal part	Side	Fragmentation	Note
C 521	5394	Passeriformes sp. indet.	ulna	dex	incomplete	
	4439		ulna	sin	fragment	carbonized
	5437	Aves indet.	vertebra		fragment	
	5356		ulna		fragment	
	5392		tarsometatarsus		fragment	juvenile
	4233		phalanga pedis		complete	
	5359		phalanga pedis		complete	subadultus
	5356		phalanga pedis (3 specimens)		complete	juvenile
	4330		phalanga pedis		fragment	
	5013		phalanga pedis		fragment	
	5264		phalanga pedis		fragment	
	4212		26 fragments		fragment	
C 644	6091	Accipitriformes sp. indet.	radius	dex	fragment	carbonized
C 704	6546	Aves indet.			fragment	
C 706	6765	*Phalacrocorax carbo*	humerus	sin	fragment	
	6765	*Anser anser*	humerus	sin	fragment	
	6765	Aves indet.			fragment	
C 714	6562	*Pelecanus onocrotalus*	carpometacarpus	dex	fragment	
C 718	6572	*Anas platyrhynchos*	tibiotarsus	sin	fragment	
C 723	6807	*Anser anser*	carpometacarpus	sin	complete	
	6802	Aves indet.	sternum		fragment	
C 755	6674	Aves indet.	tibiotarsus	sin	fragment	
C 756	6677	*Cygnus columbianus*	scapula	sin	fragment	pathological

Luncavița–Cetățuie tell (Caraș-Severin County)

This 70 by 40 m large and 7–12 m high tell settlement is located in the arch of the Danube, south of the city of Galați, north of the Măcin Mountains. The exacavations were directed by Silvia Marinescu-Bîlcu in 1998–2000. The non-avian bones were identified by Adrian Bălășescu and Valentin Radu (BĂLĂȘESCU 2003b; RADU 2003a; RADU 2003c). Only six avian finds were recovered from this site, belonging to five individuals representing the following five species: cormorant, mute swan, pintail, goshawk and crane (*Table 4*).

Năvodari–Tașaul–La Ostrov tell (Constanța County)

The 4.6 m high, ellipsoidal tell site measuring 250 by 120 m is located on the "La Ostrov" island on Lake Tașaul, near the city of Năvodari. Excavations directed by Silvia Marinescu-Bîlcu in 1999 (CIMEC 1999) yielded bird bones from the A_2 layers of the Gumelniţa culture. The non-avian remains were studied by Dragoş Moise and Valentin Radu (MOISE 2001b; RADU 2001b, RADU 2003a). The 33 identified bird bones belonged to at least 14 individuals from the following species: great-crested grebe, black-necked grebe, cormorant, mute swan, graylag goose, gadwall, mallard, pintail, tufted duck, coot and crane (*Table 4*).

Panduru tell (Tulcea County)

The site is located near the city of Baia, west of Lake Goloviţa. A total of 820 mammalian bones were identified by the head of the excavations, Dragoş Moise, in 2000 (CIMEC 2000b). Only a single bone from a medium-size duck was recognized from this settlement (*Table 4*).

4.2 Gumelniţa B_1 culture sites

Căscioarele tell (Călăraşi County)

The 5m high tell, measuring 57 by 103 m, is located on the Ostrovelul islet, near the town of Căscioarele. The site was excavated by Vladimir Dumitrescu in 1962–1965. The non-avian bones were identified by the late Alexandra Bolomey, whose results have recently been published by her Romanian archaeozoologist colleagues (BĂLĂŞESCU *et al.* 2005). The bird remains were first identified by Eugen Kessler (KESSLER 1985: 488). Having revised the 16 avian specimens, I identified the following 11 species: cormorant, grey heron, black stork/white stork, whooper swan, gray-lag goose, mallard, white-tailed eagle, lesser spotted eagle, booted eagle, crane and great bustard (*Table 4*).

Măriuţa tell (Călăraşi County)

The site is located east of Bucharest, the capital of Romania, between the Ialomiţa and the Mostiştea rivers. The settlement was excavated by Dragoş Moise in 2000, who also studied the non-avian bone remains (MOISE 2001a). There is only a very fragmented tibiotarsus from this assemblage, identified as belonging to a great bustard (*Table 4*).

Vităneşti tell (Teleorman County)

The 6.5 m high tell site, whose diameters measure 40–45 m, is located in the flood plain of the Teleorman and Vedea rivers, near the village of Purani, north of the city of Alexandria (ANDREESCU *et al.* 2003). The field campaigns, directed by Radian-Romus Andreescu between 1995–2000, yielded a rather rich avian material. The non-avian remains were studied by Adrian Bălăşescu and Valentin Radu (BĂLĂŞESCU – RADU 2003; RADU 2003a).

It is worth mentioning that a number of finds came to light from the Gumelniţa A_2 culture layers. The non-avian bones from these features have not yet been published in the first archaeozoological report (BĂLĂŞESCU *et al.* 2005: 172). Six relevant bird bones have been identified, which belonged to the following species: black grouse, crane and great bustard. A proximal humerus fragment from a crane, a sternum fragment from a female great bustard, as well as a tibiotarsus fragment from a medium-size unidentifiable bird were found in Dwelling 5 (L5/97).

The rest of the 97 bones originate from Gumelniţa B_1 features. They have been assigned to at least 27 birds from the following species: cormorant, white pelican, grey heron, whooper swan, gray-lag goose, teal, mallard, pochard/scaup, bearded vulture, pallid harrier, peregrine, black grouse, partridge, crane, Demoiselle crane, little bustard, great bustard, tawny owl, short-eared owl, fieldfare and rook/hooded crow (*Table 5*). An incomplete coracoideum from a crane was found in Dwelling 1 (L1/93). Dwelling 2 (L2/95) yielded a distal tibiotarsus from a crane and a proximal coracoideum from a male great bustard.

4.3 Cernavoda I culture sites

Hârşova tell (Constanţa County)

The approximately 1.5 m thick deposit on top of the Gumelniţa culture levels contained finds from the Cernavoda I culture (3850/3900–4000 BC; BEM 2000). The 15 bird bones found during the 1995 field season represented at least four birds from the following species: great crested grebe, unidentifiable large wading bird, mute swan/whooper swan and gray-lag goose.

4.4 Discussion

In terms of avian remains, the Chalcolithic is much better represented in South-East Romania than previous periods. In contrast to the aforementioned five Neolithic settlements, a total of ten Gumelniţa A_2, Gumelniţa B_1 and Cernavoda I culture sites yielded bird bones. Most of these remains came to light from

Gumelniţa A_2 features. It is also worth mentioning that all these Chalcolithic sites are tell settlements.

The representation of bird finds in these assemblages was rather varied. Two sites – Mariuţa and Panduru – yielded only one bone each. Assemblages from the Gumelniţa A_2 deposits at Însurăţei, Luncaviţa, Năvodari and Vităneşti, from the Gumelniţa B_1 deposits at Căscioarele and the Cernavoda I culture deposit from Hârşova were of a medium size. They yielded six to thirty-three remains, representing three to twelve identifiable species. The most abundant bird bone assemblages were excavated from Borduşani–Popină, Hârşova and the Gumelniţa A_2 features of Vităneşti (*Table 4*).

A total of 57 species were identified from the aforementioned ten sites, representing a great variety from an ecological, seasonal and ethological point of view. Most of the identified birds live in wetland and steppe environments. In addition to swans, geese, ducks, wading birds, bustards and crane, 13 species of diurnal birds of prey, including large and quite rare species such as the bearded vulture and golden eagle, as well as two owl species (tawny owl and short-eared owl) were identified. Owing to the high precision of the collection method, which involved water-sieving the sediment at some sites such as the Hârşova tell, the number of bones coming from songbirds, as well as the number of different songbird species also increased.

The grey-lag goose seems to have been the most hunted species; it was identified from seven settlements. The number of remains from this large and tasty bird was especially high at Hârşova. Cormorant and mallard were recognized from six sites each. The latter was the most preferred species at Borduşani–Popină. Crane appears to have been the third most frequently hunted bird in this period in South-East Romania. Its remains have been identified from five settlements.

The richest material of 448 remains originates from the Hârşova tell. This outstandingly high number of bird finds can be attributed to the several field seasons that were carried out, as well as the careful techniques employed during excavation. The skeletal parts from birds were rather fragmented, which resulted in 90 unidentifiable remains (Aves indet.). Thirty-four species could be recognized from the rest of the material, thus the Hârşova tell yielded the richest avifauna not only in terms of fragment numbers, but also in the number of identifiable bird bones and individuals (58).

This site is located at the top of Balta Ialomiţei Island. It is surrounded by the Romanian Lowland from the west and the Dobrogea Plateau from the east. The highest points in the latter range between 325–467 m a.s.l. The ecological characteristics of the identified fowl point to a varied environment and a balanced exploitation of these different ecotypes (*Fig. 3*). Waterfowl, as well as species characteristic of gallery forests are almost equally represented, by eleven and ten species, respectively. These bird groups include surface swimming and diving birds such as grebes, swans, ducks and coot, as well as large and small wading birds. With six species, steppe birds are the third best-represented environmental type of fowl at this site. Nevertheless, in contrast to the extremely abundant material from the grey-lag goose, the remaining species yielded a few remains that could be assigned to only one or two individuals. The absence of large steppe species such as the crane and the great bustard is noteworthy at this site.

Most of the represented woodland and forest-steppe species are birds of prey and songbirds. The great number of diurnal birds of prey from the Hârşova tell is especially noteworthy. Most of the eagles living in the territory of present-day Romania were hunted at this site. Their diverse representation must have been related to the mountainous regions of nearby Dobrogea. The remains of medium-size raptors such as the honey buzzard and the goshawk have also been found.

Considering the seasonal characteristics of birds identified from this site, the majority of species (24 = 67%) are summer visitors in South-East Romania (*Fig. 4*). Some of these (9 = 25%) may over-winter in the region during mild winters. Nine species (25%), such as the white-tailed eagle, the buzzard, the partridge and the corvids are sedentary. Bewick's swan and the whooper swan are considered only winter visitors.

Bewick's – or the tundra – swan lives in the marshlands of the tundra in North-East Europe and Siberia. The migration to wintering areas in Western Europe starts in September and continues throughout October. Small parties may appear outside the main wintering areas, e.g. on the western shore of the Black Sea. Bewick's swans return and arrive to the breeding area during February-March and May-June, respectively (CRAMP 1998). The whooper swan breeds in Iceland, Scandinavia and North Russia. The Danube Delta, as well as the Lake Razelm complex in Eastern Dobrogea are among its preferred wintering areas in the Balkans (RADU 1983: 71).

The second most abundant bird bone assemblage came to light at the Borduşani–Popină tell, located south from Hârşova, in Balta Ialomiţei. The number of remains (287), however, was hardly more than half of those recovered at Hârşova. Nevertheless, this latter site yielded a close number of individuals (50). On the other hand, the identified species are fewer than that at the previous site. Medium-size wading birds and ducks characteristic of open waters dominate

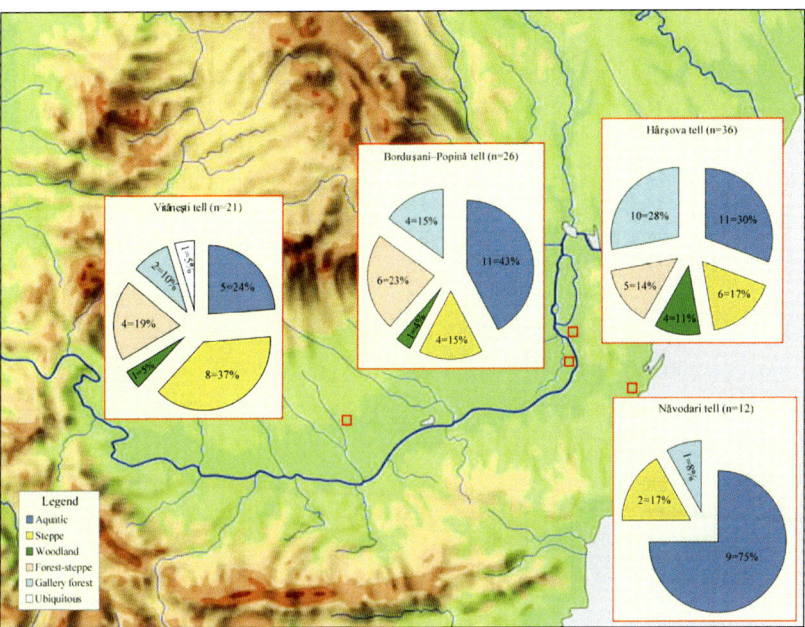

Fig. 3. Distribution of bird remains by ecotypes at the best-represented Gumelniţa culture sites in South-East Romania.

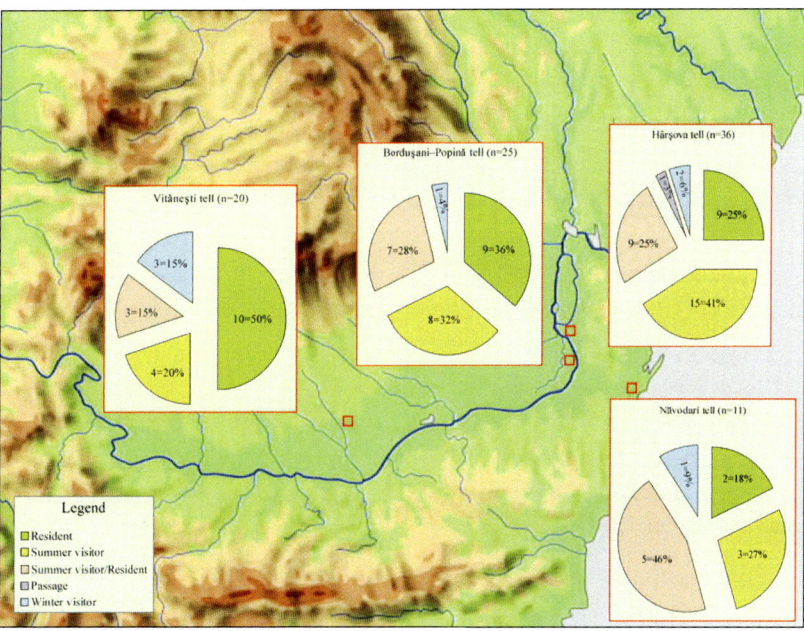

Fig. 4. Seasonal distribution of species at the best-represented Gumelniţa culture sites in South-East Romania.

by 43% among the 26 species identified. This group includes mallard, the most hunted species (45 remains from at least 6 individuals), as well as swan (26/4).

Meanwhile, birds living in steppe, forest-steppe and gallery forest habitats were equally poorly represented. Only one bone specimen was yielded by the crane and the great bustard, but the partridge and the black grouse are underrepresented as well. The booted eagle is the only species identified from Borduşani–Popină that is typical of woodlands. In addition, the white-tailed eagle and the imperial eagle were identified among the birds of prey. The hoopoe and the raven are, in general, rarely reported from archaeological sites (*Table 4*).

Considering the seasonal characteristics of the identified birds, the number of summer visitors, facultative over-wintering and sedentary species are balanced by 7–9 species each. The unossified skeletal parts originating from the chicks of a number of species (such as grey-lag goose, mallard, partridge, coot, crow and jay) hint at the exploitation of birds during the spring and summer. Only one species (teal) may be considered as a winter visitor at this site.

In contrast to the previously discussed two sites, the bird bone assemblage from the third best-represented settlement, the Vităneşti tell, has been analyzed and published here for the first time. The site is located in the southern section of the Romanian Lowland (*Fig. 1*). The 103 remains recovered belonged to 21 species and at least 31 individual birds.

The composition of identified ecotypes slightly differs from those studied so far (*Fig. 3*). Contrary to the previous two sites, steppe species were identified in the greatest number (8 species = 37%) at Vităneşti. This is the only assemblage from which both crane species occurring in Romania (crane and Demoiselle crane) were described. Also, the remains of the little bustard and the great bustard were found together in this deposit. The latter species is the second most common bird here, represented by 21 bones belonging to two males and a female.

In addition to the species living in open grassy environments, waterfowl and birds preferring forest-steppe habitats were present in greater numbers. Nevertheless, these species show greater taxonomic variability: they do not belong to certain, well defined groups as the wading birds at Hârşova or the ducks at Borduşani–Popină, for example. The best-represented species is the black grouse by 23 finds. In spite of the relatively great number of these remains, it is very likely that the bones originate from two cocks only. The occurrence of predators is also balanced at this site. Two diurnal birds of prey and two owls were identified. The bearded vulture is a rare find from archaeological deposits. Songbirds were represented by the fieldfare and the crow.

The seasonal characteristics of the identified species also differ from those of the previously discussed sites. The remains of sedentary birds dominate in the assemblage from Vităneşti, while species present only during the breeding season in South-East Romania and facultative over-wintering species are in absolute majority in the avifaunas identified at Hârşova and Borduşani–Popină (*Fig. 4*). Nevertheless, in addition to the four summer visitor species, the unossified tarsometatarsus from a grey heron also points to a summer kill. Winter visitors were represented by the whooper swan, the teal and the fieldfare. The peregrine is resident in Romania, but some specimens from northern breeding populations may also occur in the region during the winter.

The avian bone assemblage from Năvodari, although the fourth largest among the studied materials, yielded much fewer remains than the previous settlements. Its location and the identified species, however, make its short description important. The tell settlement is one of the easternmost Chalcolithic sites in Romania, located very close to the Black Sea coast. Not surprisingly, nine of the identified species are aquatic birds: two grebe species, mute swan, ducks and coot. The grey-lag goose and the crane represent the steppe species, while the cormorant indicates the presence of gallery forests in the environment.

From a seasonal point of view, the identified species are sedentary birds and summer visitors. The tufted duck is usually a winter visitor in Romania but some specimens may be found in the Danube Delta during the breeding period as well (RADU 1983: 77).

The distribution of all animal bone remains excavated from the great number of Gumelniţa culture settlements shows a diverse exploitation of natural resources and the significance of animal husbandry (*Fig. 5*). It is also worth mentioning, however, that assemblage sizes strongly differ between the sites studied, and we have no numerical data on the remains of invertebrates and fish recovered from Căscioarele during the 1960s (BĂLĂŞESCU *et al.* 2005: 173).

The exploitation of aquatic environments such as fishing and gathering is well expressed at the settlements of Borduşani–Popină, Hârşova, Luncaviţa and Năvodari, where water-sieving was applied in addition to the hand-collection of remains (*Table 1*). The amount of fish remains (more than 90% of NISP) is especially striking at Hârşova. We also have to remember, however, that the site is located directly on the bank of the Danube on the one hand, and excavations at this settlement have been carried out for the longest period of time on the other hand. These two factors also contribute to the massive presence of fish in the faunal assemblage. Wild and domestic mammals seem to have been equally exploited at Luncaviţa, while domestic animals must have provided the basic meat resource for the inhabitants of Borduşani–Popină and Năvodari, especially during the cold seasons when shellfish and fish were less easily available.

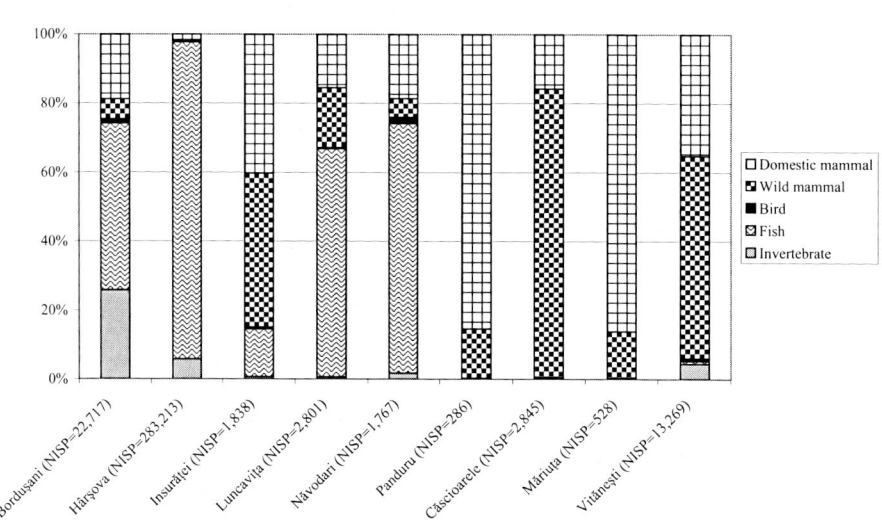

Fig. 5. Percentual distributions of the number of identifiable specimens (NISP) of the main animal groups at the Gumelniţa culture sites in South-East Romania.

It is likely that hunting was an important activity at Căscioarele and Vitănești, where the proportion of wild animal remains is over 60%. It has been mentioned, however, that aquatic animals were also identified from Căscioarele, a site rather close to the Danube, but the number of these remains is not available (BĂLĂŞESCU et al. 2005: 173).

The bone assemblage excavated from one of the sites located most inland, Vitănești, is the third largest representing this archaeological period. Although the great number of bones from red deer (*Cervus elaphus* Linnaeus, 1758) and wild boar (*Sus scrofa* Linnaeus, 1758) point to the greater exploitation of forest faunas, hunting in steppe habitats is also indicated by the remains of aurochs (*Bos primigenius* Bojanus, 1827), equids (BĂLĂŞESCU – RADU 2003; BĂLĂŞESCU et al. 2005) and birds (*Fig. 3*). In addition to the major contribution of waterfowl discussed in this study, hunting in the marshland along the floodplain of the Teleorman river is confirmed by the relatively great number of bones from beaver (*Castor fiber* Linnaeus, 1758). Contrary to the distribution of finds from the Boian culture site of Isaccea–Suhat, where the dominance of remains from wild animals seems to be correlated to the relative abundance of dog remains, bones from this species make up less than 3% of the mammalian assemblage at Vităneşti. This observation would again suggest that dog complemented the meat provision of certain hunting societies only in the Neolithic (BARTOSIEWICZ 2005: 53–54).

Wild- and domestic mammals were equally well represented at the other inland site, Însurăţei. In addition, fishing must have been seasonally practiced. The remains of domestic animals dominated the two smallest assemblages excavated from Panduru and Măriuţa (*Fig. 5*).

The avian remains made up only a small portion of the bone assemblages under discussion here and were rather under-represented in comparison with the remains of fish or mammals in both periods. Nevertheless, when their taxonomic richness is compared to that of wild mammals, birds seem to be better represented in taxonomic terms. In *Figure 6*, the decimal logarithms of the number of mammalian and avian taxa (R = y) are plotted against the decimal logarithms of their respective numbers of identifiable specimens (NISP = x). The diagram reflects how taxonomic richness increases with the number of specimens identified in the larger Chalcolithic assemblages of a better representative value.

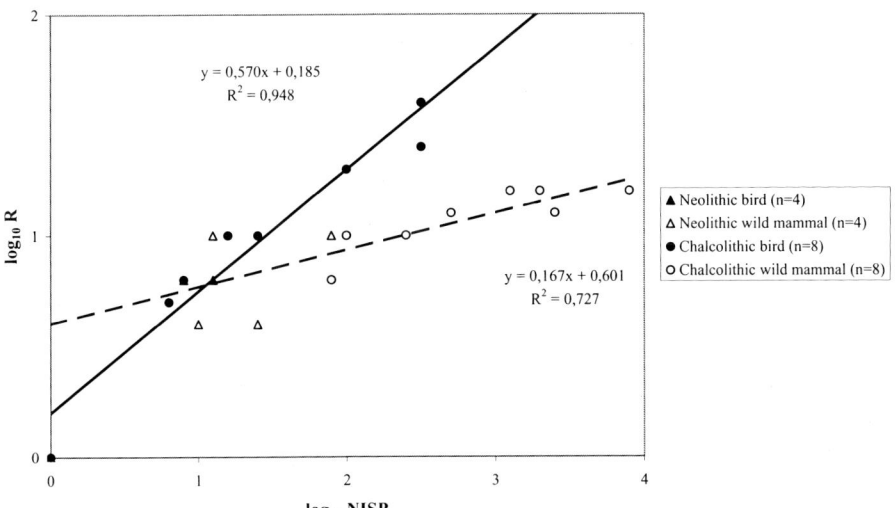

Fig. 6. Relationship between the number of identifiable specimens (NISP, x) and the number of species identified (R, y) in the Neolithic and Chalcolithic bone assemblages from South-East Romania. Continuous trend line: Chalcolithic birds; dashed trend line: Chalcolithic mammals.

Nevertheless, although both highly significant ($P \leq 0.005$), the two relationships shown for Chalcolithic bird and game are described by different linear regression equations. Since the number of large mammalian species (found even in recent faunas) is much smaller than that of birds, increasing the size of bone assemblages will provide new species in a smaller degree than in the case of birds. The smaller repertoire of mammalian species of archaeological interest will also be exhausted at a certain point. Countering this result, even scarce avian assemblages are rather diverse in species and this richness strongly increases with the number of remains identified.

5. Bird Remains from Neolithic Sites in the Great Hungarian Plain

5.1 Körös culture sites

Ecsegfalva 23 (Békés County)

This site is located in the region of the Körös and Berettyó rivers in the Great Hungarian Plain, north of the town of Gyomaendrőd. The Ecsegfalva excavation was undertaken as a joint project by the Institute of Archaeology (Hungarian Academy of Sciences, Budapest), Békés County Museum, Munkácsy Mihály Museum (Békéscsaba), and Cardiff University (UK). Excavations between 1998–2001 were directed by Alasdair Whittle. Radiocarbon analyses suggest a 5900–5500 calBC date for this early Neolithic settlement (Whittle *et al.* 2002). One of the richest Körös culture animal bone assemblages came to light from this site, owing in part to systematic water-sieving. The results have been partially published (PIKE-TAY *et al.* 2004). Additional details are forthcoming (BARTOSIEWICZ 2007a; BARTOSIEWICZ 2007b; GÁL 2007b; PIKE-TAY 2007).

A total of 276 complete and fragmented bird remains belonged to at least 61 individuals. Of the 52 taxa recognized, 40 could be identified to the level of species: great crested grebe, bittern, night heron, great white egret, grey heron, purple heron, spoonbill, grey-lag goose, gadwall, teal, mallard, pintail, garganey, garganey/shoveler, pochard, ferruginous duck, tufted duck, goosander, unidentifiable harrier, goshawk, buzzard, booted eagle, black grouse, partridge, spotted crake, moorhen, coot, crane, great bustard, woodcock, black-tailed godwit, woodpigeon, tawny owl, roller, great spotted woodpecker, skylark, blackbird, mistle thrush, unidentifiable warbler, jay, magpie, rook/hooded crow, starling and house sparrow (*Table 7*).

Endrőd 39, Endrőd 119 and Endrőd 3/6 (Békés County)

The "Endrőd" sites formed a series of occupations in the vicinity of Gyomaendrőd, on the edge of the floodplain of the Körös river. During several decades of excavations in the second half of the 20th century, a total of 226 sites were found here in a microregion of approximately 42 km^2, encompassing 11 archaeological periods (BÖKÖNYI 1992b).

Excavations at both of the Körös culture sites, Endrőd 39 and Endrőd 119, were directed by János Makkay (MAKKAY 1992). Radiocarbon dates for Endrőd 39

Table 7. List of bird taxa identified from Körös culture sites in the Great Hungarian Plain (NISP/MNI). Site numbers:
1. Ecsegfalva 23; 2. Endrőd 3/6; 3. Endrőd 39; 4. Endrőd 119; 5. Kötelek–Huszársarok; 6. Maroslele–Pana; 7. Nagykörű–Tsz.; 8. Őszentiván (Tiszasziget); 9. Röszke–Ludvár; 10. Szajol–Felsőföld; 11. Szolnok–Szanda; 12. Tiszaszőlős–Domaháza–Puszta.

Taxon		Habitat	Seasonality	Food	1	2	3	4	5	6	7	8	9	10	11	12
Gavia arctica	Black-throated diver	A	P/WV	C					1							
Tachybaptus ruficollis	Little grebe	A	SV/R	C						1						
Podiceps cristatus	Great crested grebe	A	SV/R	C	5/1	3/2				3	1					
Podiceps cf. auritus	Slavonian grebe	A	WV	C				1								
Phalacrocorax carbo	Cormorant	GF	SV	C		5/2							1			
Pelecanus onocrotalus	White pelican	A	SV/P	C						1						
Botaurus stellaris	Bittern	A	SV/R	C	2/1	1										
Nycticorax nycticorax	Night heron	GF	SV	C	2/1											1
Egretta garzetta	Little egret	GF	SV	C		1		1								
Egretta alba	Great white egret	A	SV/R	C	2/1	1		3		2	6/3	1				1
Ardea cinerea	Grey heron	GF	SV/R	C	4/2	6/2	2	1	1	1	7/1		6			2/1
Ardea purpurea	Purple heron	A	SV	C	8/1		1						4			
Ciconia cf. nigra	Black stork	GF	SV	C				2					3	1		
Ciconia cf. ciconia	White stork	FS	SV	C									2			
Ciconia nigra/C. ciconia	Black stork/White stork	GF/FS	SV	C		7/2	1				8/3					1
Platalea leucorodia	Spoonbill	A	SV	C	2/1			1								
Ciconiiformes sp. indet.	unidentifiable wading bird										5/?				1	
Cygnus olor	Mute swan	A	SV/**WV**	H		11/3		2								
Anser fabalis	Bean goose	S	P/WV	H			1			3					1	
Anser albifrons	White-fronted goose	S	P/WV	H				2		3		1				
Anser anser	Grey-lag goose	S	SV	H	4/2	5/1	2	1			8/1			1	3	
Anser sp.	unidentifiable goose	S	?	H		1					1					
Branta leucopsis	Barnacle goose	S	WV	H							1					1

Taxon		Habitat	Seasonality	Food	1	2	3	4	5	6	7	8	9	10	11	12
Anas cf. penelope	Wigeon	A	P	O			1									3/2
Anas cf. strepera	Gadwall	A	SV/P	O	6/3											
Anas crecca	Teal	A	P	O	8/1	5/3										
Anas platyrhynchos	Mallard	A	SV/R	O	33/6	41/7	19	12		4	7/3		11	1	8	4/1
Anas aff. acuta	Pintail	A	SV/P	O	3/1											
Anas querquedula	Garganey	A	SV/P	O	6/2	2/1										
Anas cf. clypeata	Shoveler	A	SV/P	O	1	7/2		1								
Anas sp.	unidentified duck	A	?	O	11/?	11/?				1				1		
Aythya ferina	Pochard	A	SV/R	O	3/1	1		6		1	1					
Aythya nyroca	Ferruginous duck	A	SV/R	O	17/3	2/1		3			1		2			1
Aythya fuligula	Tufted duck	A	P/WV	O	2/1								1			
Aythya marila	Scaup	A	P	O												1
Mergus cf. merganser	Goosander	A	WV	C	1											
Anseriformes sp. indet.	unidentifiable waterfowl				21/?	2/?										1
Haliaeetus albicilla	White-tailed eagle	GF	R	C									2		1	
Circaetus gallicus	Short-toed eagle	W	SV	C									1			
Circus aeruginosus	Marsh harrier	A	SV/R	C									2			
Circus sp.	unidentifiable harrier	?	?		1											
Buteo buteo	Buzzard	FS	R	C	1											
Aquila pomarina	Lesser spotted eagle	GF	SV	C												1
Hieraaetus pennatus	Booted eagle	W	SV	C	1		1	7								
Tetrao tetrix	Black grouse	FS	R	O	2/1			1								
Perdix perdix	Partridge	S	R	O	1											
Porzana porzana	Spotted crake	A	SV/R	C	1											
Gallinula chloropus	Moorhen	GF	SV	C	1											1
Fulica atra	Coot	A	SV/R	C	14/2	2/1	3	1		2	2/1	2/?	1			6/2

Taxon		Habitat	Seasonality	Food	1	2	3	4	5	6	7	8	9	10	11	12
Grus grus	Crane	S	SV/P	C	1		3	6	2/1	1			1			
Tetrax tetrax	Little bustard	S	R	C				2							2	
Otis tarda	Great bustard	S	R	C	1		14	8						1	2	
Scolopax rusticola	Woodcock	W	SVP	C	1											
Limosa limosa	Black-tailed godwit	S	SV/P	C	1											
Larus cf. argentatus	Herring gull	A	V	C												
Columba palumbus	Woodpigeon	W	SV/R	H	24/4					2			1			1
Strix aluco	Tawny owl	W	R	C	1											
Coracias garrulus	Roller	FS	SV	C	1			1								
Dendrocopus major	Great spotted woodpecker	W	R	1	1											
Alauda arvensis	Skylark	S	SV/R	1	1											
Turdus merula	Blackbird	W	R	O	1											
Turdus viscivorus	Mistle trush	W	R/WV	O	1											
Turdus sp.	unidentifiable trush	W	?	O	2/?											
Acrocephalus sp.	unidentifiable warbler	A	?	1	1											
Garrulus glandarius	Jay	W	R		1											
Pica pica	Magpie	FS	R	O												
Corvus cf. frugilegus	Rook	FS	R	O			2									
Corvus cf. corone	Carrion crow	FS	R	O												
Corvus frugilegus/C. corone	Rook/Carrion crow	FS	R	O	2/1					1						
Sturnus vulgaris	Starling	FS	SV/R	O	6/2										1	
Passer domesticus	House sparrow	FS	R	O	2/2											
Passeriformes indet.	unidentifiable passerine	?	?	?	5/?											
Aves indet.	unidentifiable bird	?	?	?	59/?	14		545		1	3					10
Total					276/61	127/31	53	607	4/3	27	51/19	4/?	38	5	19	35/16

range from 5930–5520 calBC and 6200–5550 calBC, respectively (WHITTLE *et al.* 2005). Endrőd 119 was dated to 5900–5500 calBC (WHITTLE *et al.* 2002). Excavations at the multi-period site of Endrőd 3/6 were completed by Dénes Jankovich-Bésán and János Makkay between 1974–1986 (MAKKAY 2007).

According to Sándor Bökönyi, fish and bird bones were more frequent than mammalian remains at Endrőd 39 (BÖKÖNYI 1989: 14). The total of 53 avian bones belonged to the following 12 species: grey heron, purple heron, spoonbill, bean goose, grey-lag goose, wigeon, mallard, black grouse, coot, crane, great bustard and rook (JÁNOSSY 1985: 68).

The fish and mammalian remains from Endrőd 119 were identified by István TAKÁCS (1992) and Sándor BÖKÖNYI (1992a), respectively. This site yielded the greatest ever number of bird bones from a prehistoric settlement in Hungary. The majority (90%) of 545 fragments, however, were unidentifiable. The remaining 62 bones represented 20 species: Slavonian grebe, little egret, great white egret, grey heron, black stork, spoonbill, mute swan, white-fronted goose, grey-lag goose, mallard, shoveler, pochard, ferruginous duck, black grouse, partridge, coot, crane, little bustard, great bustard and tawny owl (BÖKÖNYI 1992a: 198). The bird remains from this site were identified by Dénes Jánossy.

Bird bones from the site of Endrőd 3/6 originate from two features. The first assemblage, including 29 specimens from at least 11 birds, was excavated from the southern part of the Western pit in Trench XVIII, at the depth of 110–135 cm. The second assemblage (98 remains from 25 individuals) came to light from Pit 4c of Trench VIII. The stratigraphy of this site is rather complex, since a semi-subterranean house had been dug into the Körös, the Alföld Linear Pottery and (to a smaller extent) the Tiszapolgár culture pits during the Late Copper Age. According to the pottery-based chronology of the site, both avian assemblages date to the end of the Körös period (MAKKAY 2007). Therefore, the identified species, which represent at least 31 individuals, are listed together: great crested grebe, cormorant, bittern, little egret, great white egret, grey heron, black stork/white stork, mute swan, grey-lag goose, teal, mallard, garganey, shoveler, pochard, ferruginous duck and coot.

Kőtelek–Huszársarok (Jász-Nagykun-Szolnok County)

The site, which extends 4 km south-west of the village of Kőtelek, on the former floodplain of the Tisza river, was excavated by Pál Raczky in 1974 (RACZKY 1975). The non-avian animal remains were identified by István Vörös (VÖRÖS 1980). Five bird bones found in the Körös culture Feature 1 were identified by

Dénes Jánossy. Four bones were assigned to the black-throated diver, the grey heron and the crane (JÁNOSSY 1985: 71). In addition, a bird bone was also found in one of the ALPC features (see below).

Maroslele–Pana (Csongrád County)

The site is located on a small, former island on the north side of the Maros river valley. The small-scale rescue excavations were directed by Ottó Trogmayer in 1963. Radiocarbon analyses yielded a 6440–6230 calBC date for this settlement (WHITTLE *et al.* 2005). The scarce non-avian remains that could be recovered were studied by Sándor Bökönyi (BÖKÖNYI 1964: 81). The 27 bird bones were identified by Dénes Jánossy. They represented the following species: little grebe, great crested grebe, white pelican, great white egret, grey heron, bean goose, white-fronted goose, mallard, pochard, coot, crane, herring gull and rook/hooded crow (JÁNOSSY 1985: 71).

Nagykörű–Tsz. (Jász-Nagykun-Szolnok County)

This site, excavated on the outskirts of the village of Nagykörű, was discovered following the plantation of fruit-trees during the late 1960s. Recent archaeological excavations, directed by Pál Raczky, have been limited to a 3 by 3 m, approximately 1.5 m deep test pit. As a result of water-sieving, this small excavation yielded approximately 800 vertebrate remains. The non-avian bones were identified by László Bartosiewicz (RACZKY *et al.* 2007). Fifty-one finds belonged to birds. These could be assigned to at least 17 individuals from the following 12 taxa: great crested grebe, great white egret, grey heron, black stork/white stork, grey-lag goose, barnacle goose, mallard, pochard, ferruginous duck and coot. The detailed description of the material is given in a separate article (RACZKY *et al.* 2007).

Ószentiván (Tiszasziget) (Csongrád County)

The multi-period settlement, located south of the city of Szolnok, was excavated by Ida Kutzián in 1960. Recent radiocarbon analyses yielded a 5560–5290 calBC date for the Körös culture habitation of the settlement (WHITTLE *et al.* 2005). These features yielded four bird bones that were identified by Dénes Jánossy. They originated from the following species: great white egret, white-fronted goose and coot (JÁNOSSY 1985: 71).

Röszke–Lúdvár (Csongrád County)

The settlement, discovered on an elevation of the Tisza floodplain, is located south of the village of Röszke. The site was excavated by Ottó Trogmayer in 1964–1965. In addition to the remains of a house model, idols and pottery, a special bone assemblage was also found in a large pit (TROGMAYER 1965a: 18). Marks of burning discovered at the edge of this feature indicate that the ancient population had used it as a clay extraction pit (TROGMAYER 1965b: 15). The absolute age of this site falls between 5930–5720 calBC (WHITTLE *et al.* 2005). The non-avian bones were studied by Sándor Bökönyi (BÖKÖNYI 1974: 396). The large refuse pits also contained 38 bird bones. They were identified by Dénes Jánossy as those of cormorant, grey heron, purple heron, black stork, white stork, mallard, ferruginous duck, tufted duck, white-tailed eagle, short-toad eagle, marsh harrier, coot, crane and woodpigeon (JÁNOSSY 1985: 72–73).

Szajol–Felsőföld (Jász-Nagykun-Szolnok County)

Rescue excavations conducted by Pál Raczky in 1976 unearthed an approximately 500 by 200 m large Körös culture settlement on the former bank of the Tisza river. A rather poor animal bone assemblage was brought to light from this site. The non-avian remains were identified by István Vörös (VÖRÖS 1980: 46–47). The five avian remains, found in the dwelling house and nearby refuse pit, were identified by Dénes Jánossy as representing the following species: grey-lag goose, mallard, black stork and great bustard (JÁNOSSY 1985: 73).

Szolnok–Szanda (Jász-Nagykun-Szolnok County)

This rather large site, covering 287.5 m^2, is located south of the city of Szolnok. It was excavated by Nándor Kalicz and Pál Raczky in 1978. The features uncovered here included the remains of two burnt down houses. The animal bones were brought to light from the fill of pits located outside and underneath of the dwellings. The nineteen avian remains were identified by Dénes Jánossy. They included the bones of spoonbill, bean goose, grey-lag goose, mallard, white-tailed eagle, crane, great bustard and hooded crow (JÁNOSSY 1985: 73).

Tiszaszőlős–Domaháza–Puszta–Réti-dűlő (Jász-Nagykun-Szolnok County)

The excavations directed by László Domboróczki in 2003 uncovered a small (20 by 30 m) Körös culture settlement within the larger multi-period site. It lay on the bank of the former flood plain of the Tisza, in the south-eastern outskirts of Tiszaörvény, today forming part of the city of Tiszafüred (DOMBORÓCZKY

2004). The significance of this site is attributed to the fact that Tiszaszőlős–Domaháza-puszta–Réti-dűlő is the northernmost Körös culture settlement known in the Middle Tisza region to date (Domboróczki pers. comm.). The non-avian bones were identified by István Vörös. The 35 bird remains represented at least 16 individuals from the following species: night heron, great white egret, grey heron, black stork/white stork, grey-lag goose, wigeon, mallard, ferruginous duck, scaup, lesser spotted eagle, moorhen, coot and woodpigeon.

5.2 Alföld Linear Pottery culture sites

Debrecen–Nyulas (Hajdú-Bihar County)

Small scale rescue excavations have been carried out along the edge of the main road leading from the city of Debrecen to Hajdúböszörmény by János Dani in 2005. The Neolithic settlement that yielded four avian bones once occupied the slight elevation on the southern bank of Tócó creek, today flowing some 150–200 m north of the site (DANI 2007). The non-avian animal bones were identified by László Bartosiewicz (BARTOSIEWICZ 2007c). Only four bird bones have been found in the assemblage, representing the following species: purple heron, grey-lag goose and woodpigeon.

Kőtelek–Huszársarok (Jász-Nagykun-Szolnok County)

In addition to the aforementioned Körös culture assemblage, the site also provided a single bird bone from a pit assigned to the Szatmár II Group. It was identified as crane (JÁNOSSY 1985: 71). New radiocarbon dates indicate that the Early Alföld Linear Pottery culture occupation at the site fell to between 5720–5530 calBC (RACZKY et al. 2007).

Tiszavalk–Négyesi határ (Borsod-Abaúj-Zemplén County)

This prehistoric settlement is located on the western outskirts of the village of Tiszavalk. A single feature was unearthed here by Pál Patay in 1968. In addition to the finds characteristic of the Körös culture, the fragment of an idol with a triangular face was also discovered (PATAY 1969: 23). Only a single bird bone, belonging to coot, was found (JÁNOSSY 1985: 74–75).

Tiszavasvári– Keresztfal (Szabolcs-Szatmár-Bereg County)

Rescue excavations at this settlement were directed by János Makkay and Nándor Kalicz in 1962 and 1963, respectively. A large (8 by 3 m) pit containing domestic refuse was found in 1963 that included a great number of potsherds, animal bones and bone artifacts. Among the latter, a projectile point was described (KALICZ 1964).

The non-avian bones were identified by Sándor Bökönyi (BÖKÖNYI 1974: 417). Only a single bird bone derives from this bone assemblage, assigned to a spoonbill (JÁNOSSY 1985: 74).

5.3 Bükk–Szilmeg culture sites

Polgár–Folyás (Folyás– Szilmeg) (Hajdú-Bihar County)

The small-scale excavations directed by Ida Bognár Kutzián at Tiszapolgár in 1950 yielded a small number of animal bones. The non-avian remains were identified by Sándor Bökönyi (BÖKÖNYI 1959: 49). Only one bird bone was discovered in the material, identified as crane (JÁNOSSY 1985: 70).

5.4 Tisza culture sites

Kisköre–Gát (Heves County)

The site was excavated by József Korek between 1963–1965, within the framework of a rescue project preceding the constructions of the dam system along the Tisza. The settlement was found on the north-eastern part of the hillock, located between the modern embankment and the former riverbed (KOREK 1977: 3). A rather small animal bone assemblage was brought to light. The non-avian bones were identified by Sándor Bökönyi (BÖKÖNYI 1974: 375). The two bird bones, found in Pit 1 which was actually a dwelling, were identified by Dénes Jánossy as black stork (JÁNOSSY 1985: 70).

Szegvár–Tűzköves (Csongrád County)

This site was also excavated by József Korek in 1970. Twenty-eight burials, as well as four disturbed dwellings, were unearthed at this location (KOREK 1971). The animal bone material was rather scarce. The non-avian finds were identified by Sándor Bökönyi (BÖKÖNYI 1959: 48–49). The three bird remains were identified as belonging to a pelican species, a goose species and the white-tailed eagle (JÁNOSSY 1985: 73).

Szerencs–Taktaföldvár (Borsod-Abaúj-Zemplén County)

The site is located on a small hill in the marshland, some 3 km from the city of Szerencs, near Takta brook. The remains of dwellings and pits, as well as a human skeleton buried in a contracted position, were unearthed by Tibor Kemenczei in 1967. A five-barbed antler harpoon was also found in the rich bone assemblage (KEMENCZEI 1968).

The non-avian remains were identified by István Vörös (VÖRÖS 1986a: 119). Only four bird bones were found at this site, representing the grey-lag goose and the white-tailed eagle (JÁNOSSY 1985: 73).

5.5 Herpály–Csőszhalom culture sites

Berettyószentmárton (Hajdú-Bihar County)

The tell settlement located in the valley of the Berettyó river, south of the village of Berettyóújfalu, was excavated by Ida Bognár-Kutzián and Nándor Kalicz in 1954–1955. It yielded a rather abundant animal bone assemblage that was studied by Sándor Bökönyi. Two avian remains were found that were identified as belonging to a duck species (BÖKÖNYI 1959: 53–55) and the white-tailed eagle (JÁNOSSY 1985: 68).

Polgár–Csőszhalom (Tiszapolgár) (Hajdú-Bihar County)

The settlement, including the remains of burnt down houses and burials, was excavated by Ida Bognár Kutzián in 1957 (B. KUTZIÁN 1958). The non-avian animal bones were identified by Sándor Bökönyi (BÖKÖNYI 1974: 394). Recent studies on the food refuse and bone artifacts have been completed by Charles A. Schwartz and Alice M. Choyke (SCHWARTZ 1998; CHOYKE 2001). Three bird bones are known from this site, representing the purple heron and the eagle owl (JÁNOSSY 1985: 72).

5.6 Discussion

Excavations at Neolithic settlements in Eastern Hungary yielded rather abundant information on birds (GÁL 2004). It is noteworthy that the Körös culture is extremely well represented both in terms of the number of sites and the number of bone specimens recovered. Although it is likely that fowling indeed played an important role in the life of ancient people at the beginning of the Neolithic, other factors also contributed to the forming of representative assemblages. The Hungarian archaeozoologist Sándor Bökönyi dedicated many years to the study of Körös culture assemblages when investigating the beginnings of animal husbandry in the Carpathian Basin. This resulted in a major body of archaeozoological information on the Early Neolithic. In addition, the current interest in a multidisciplinary approach to archaeology has resulted in the introduction of new excavation methods. Of these, wet and dry sieving have a direct impact on the efficient recovery of small finds, such as the bones of fish and bird, as well as archaeobotanical remains.

Since the Early Neolithic is represented by a single culture in Hungary (the Körös culture in the Great Hungarian Plain) and because the number of avian, as well as non-avian, bone assemblages from these settlements are incomparably more abundant than those from the Middle and Late Neolithic, this period calls for a close scrutiny.

Altogether 62 bird species have been identified from 12 Körös culture settlements (*Table 7*). A number of taxa could be identified to the level of genus or family only. The average bird bone assemblage consists of 2 to 36 remains per site. However, the number of recovered bird bones varies widely, from 4 to 607 per site. The richest assemblage was brought to light at Endrőd 119, but only 10% of the bird remains could be identified. Thus the recently excavated site of Ecsegfalva 23 may be considered the most abundant with the 276 specimens, 40 species and at least 61 individuals that have been identified (GÁL 2007b).

Approximately 50% of the identified avian species live in wetland environments. They include several aquatic species (e.g. grebes, ducks, coot and gull) and wading birds (herons, egrets, storks). Some of the latter species and a number of diurnal birds of prey (e.g. the white-tailed eagle and lesser spotted eagle), as well as other species, such as the cormorant and moorhen, prefer gallery forests for nesting. Several steppe species (e.g. geese) also favour grassland habitats near wetlands. The most frequently hunted birds in the Early Neolithic represent these ecotypes: the mallard has been identified at ten sites, while the grey heron and the coot at nine sites each. The grey-lag goose was identified at eight settlements, while the great white egret and the crane at seven sites each (*Table 7*).

In contrast with the dominance of waterfowl, only a few bird taxa are indicative of bird exploitation in dry steppe habitats during this period. The most frequent species representing this type of environment is the great bustard, recognized at five sites. Both the little and the great bustard, as well as other dry and wet steppe birds, were identified from Endrőd 119, where altogether 6 species (30%) belonged to this ecotype. Birds living in the woodland and forest-steppe are frequent, but one has to take into account that a great number of passerines and other small birds belong to this group (*Fig. 7*). Most of these species have been identified from Ecsegfalva 23 only, as a result of unusually cautious excavation, especially the use of water-sieving.

Summer visitors and resident species, that is, birds breeding in the Great Hungarian Plain, are best represented at these Early Neolithic sites (*Fig. 8*). Very few winter visitors, such as the Slavonian grebe (Endrőd 119), the barnacle goose (Nagykörű–Tsz.) and the goosander (Ecsegfalva 23) have been identified. A number of species, such as the black-throated grebe (Kőtelek–Huszársarok), the bean goose (Endrőd 39, Maroslele–Pana and Szolnok–Szanda), the white-fronted goose (Endrőd 119, Maroslele–Pana and Ószentiván) and the tufted duck (Ecsegfalva 23 and Röszke–Lúdvár) pass through Hungary during their migration periods and sometimes also over-winter in the area. Some populations of the mistle thrush (Ecsegfalva 23) breed in Hungary, while some of the northern populations only over-winter in this region. Ornithological data support the view that the white pelican and the mute swan used to breed in Hungary until the recent past; today they are passage and winter visitor species, respectively (PETERSON *et al.* 1977).

Earlier (BÖKÖNYI 1974: 21–30) and more recent archaeozoological investigations (BARTOSIEWICZ 2005) offer evidence that meat provisioning during the Early Neolithic was based on animal husbandry in the Carpathian Basin. In spite of the humid and cool environment of the often flooded plains, the numbers of sheep – and to some extent goat – remains usually far exceed those of cattle and other domestic animals (BARTOSIEWICZ 2005, Table 1; BARTOSIEWICZ 2007a, Table 6). These are indicative of a strong agricultural tradition of south-eastern roots practiced by the people settled in the Carpathian Basin during the 7th millennium.

This general picture may be seen in *Fig. 9*, which illustrates the share of avian and mammalian bones at the sites from which relevant data were available. Although a great number of fish remains have been collected from the sites of Ecsegfalva 23 and Endrőd 119 (almost 18,000 and 592, respectively; the latter

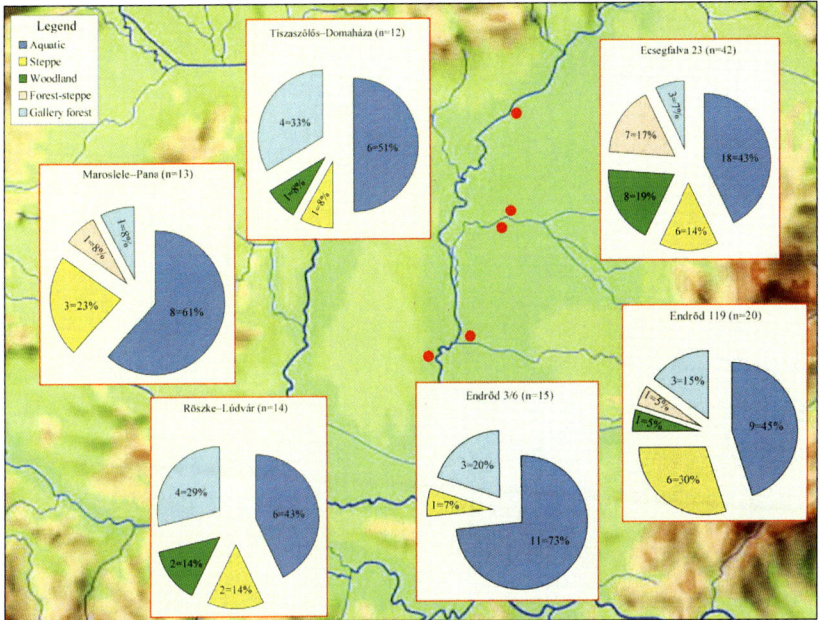

Fig. 7. Distribution of bird remains by ecotypes at the best-represented Körös culture sites in the Great Hungarian Plain.

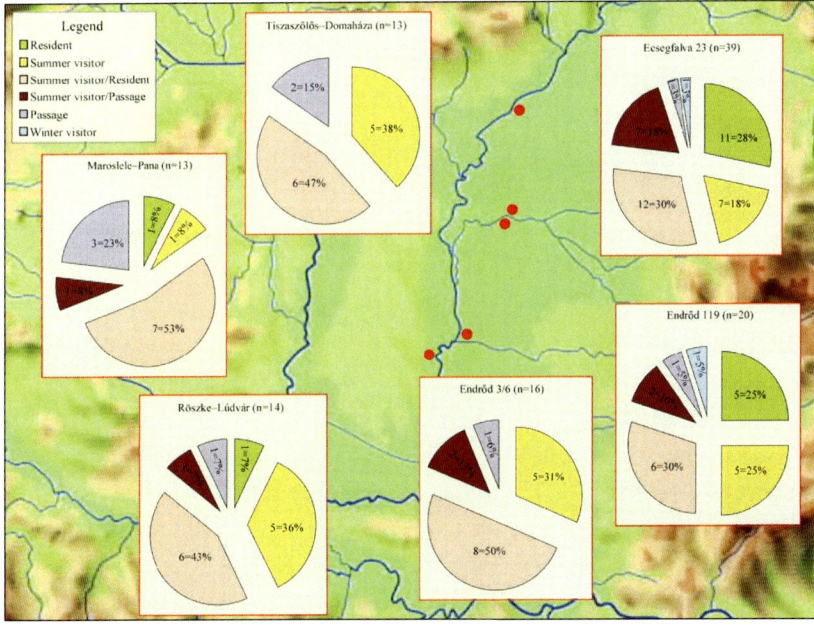

Fig. 8. Seasonal distribution of species at the best-represented Körös culture sites in the Great Hungarian Plain.

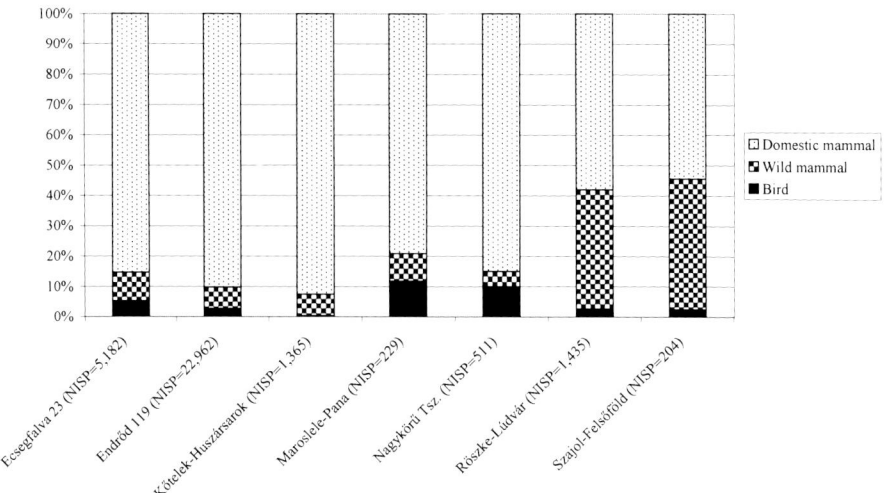

Fig. 9. Percentual distributions of the number of identifiable specimens (NISP) of the main animal groups at Körös culture sites in the Great Hungarian Plain.

by hand), this class of vertebrates (TAKÁCS 1992; BARTOSIEWICZ 2007b) is not included in the present analysis because the incomplete data would have distorted the diagram. It has to be kept in mind that most sites under discussion in this chapter were excavated in the second half of the 20th century and the bone remains were exclusively hand-collected.

It is worth mentioning that the contribution of bird bones reaches and even exceeds 10% of the entire bone assemblage at the sites of Nagykörű–Tsz. and Maroslele–Pana. These sites yielded, however, rather small bone assemblages, with only 511 and 229 remains, respectively. Similarly scarce material is known from the settlement of Szajol–Felsőföld, where avian remains represent less than 3%. This small contribution of bird bones is characteristic of Körös sites, and it does not seem to be closely related to the range of wild animals noted at some settlements such as Röszke–Lúdvár and Szajol–Felsőföld.

Among the later sites, ten Middle and Late Neolithic settlements yielded bird remains in the Great Hungarian Plain. The two periods are similarly represented by the four Alföld Linear Pottery culture settlements and one Bükk-Szilmeg culture settlement, as well as the three Tisza and two Herpály-Csőszhalom culture settlements. All the bone assemblages excavated from these sites are extremely poor in avian remains, and are represented by no more than one to four bones per site (*Table 8*).

Table 8. List of bird taxa identified from Middle and Late Neolithic sites in Hungary (NISP/MNI).

Site numbers: 1. Debrecen–Nyulas; 2. Kötelek–Huszársarok 3. Tiszavalk–Négyesi-határ; 4. Tiszavasvári–Keresztfal; 5. Polgár–Folyás; 6. Kisköre–Gát; 7. Szegvár–Tűzköves; 8. Szerencs–Taktaföldvár; 9. Berettyószentmárton; 10. Polgár–Csőszhalom.

Taxon		Habitat	Seasonality	Food	Middle Neolithic					Late Neolithic				
					Alföld Linear Pottery				Bükk-Szilmeg	Tisza			Herpály-Csőszhalom	
					1	2	3	4	5	6	7	8	9	10
Pelecanus sp.	unidentifiable pelican	A		C										
Ardea purpurea	Purple heron	A	SV	C	1									1
Ciconia cf. nigra	Black stork	GF	SV	C						2/1				
Platalea leucorodia	Spoonbill	A	SV	C				1						
Anser anser	Grey-lag goose	S	SV	H	1							3/1		
Anser sp.	unidentifiable goose	S		H							1			
Anas sp.	unidentifiable duck	A	?	O		1							1	
Haliaeetus albicilla	White-tailed eagle	GF	R	C							1	1	1	
Fulica atra	Coot	A	SV/R	C			1							
Grus grus	Crane	S	SV/P	C					1					
Columba palumbus	Woodpigeon	W	SV/R	H	1									
Bubo bubo	Eagle owl	W	R	C										1
Aves indet.	unidentifiable birds	?	?	?	1			1	1					1
Total					4	1	1	1	1	2/1	3/3	4/2	2/2	3/3

63

A total of 12 bird taxa have been recognized from the Middle and Late Neolithic sites under discussion here. Nine of these could be identified to the level of species and three to the level of genus. As with Körös culture assemblages, the remains of waterfowl and birds living in the proximity of wetlands were encountered most frequently. Geese and crane, on the other hand, represent a steppe environment. Only two forest species, woodpigeon (Debrecen–Nyulas) and eagle owl (Polgár–Csőszhalom) have been identified. The white-tailed eagle seems to have been commonly hunted; its bones were recorded at three sites.

The majority of the identified birds arrive to Hungary only during the breeding season. Nevertheless, some of them, such as the coot and the woodpigeon, may over-winter in the Great Hungarian Plain during mild winters if there is available food. Among the birds known from this period only a single species, the eagle owl, is characteristic of the Hungarian avifauna throughout the year.

The non-avian bone assemblages available from Middle and Late Neolithic sites are also poor. Fish bones were collected only from five settlements (Tiszavasvári–Keresztfal, Polgár–Folyás, Szegvár–Tűzköves, Szerencs–Taktaföldvár and Polgár–Csőszhalom). Since the excavation methods applied at the different settlements differed and water-sieving was practiced only exceptionally, the excavated fish remains were underrepresented (1 to 15 remains per site). Therefore, similarly to Early Neolithic (Körös culture) settlements, I have decided not to include them in this work.

Similarly to the Early Neolithic, most of the meat was provided by domestic animals at the majority of Middle and Late Neolithic sites (*Fig. 10*). However, an increase in wild animal remains may be observed, beginning with the Tisza culture. This tendency is already visible at the Polgár–Folyás site (Bükk-Szilmeg culture). The bones of wild mammals clearly dominate the two Late Neolithic (Herpály-Csőszhalom culture) settlements, Berettyószentmárton and Polgár–Csőszhalom. The analysis of mammalian assemblages from 53 Neolithic settlements outlined a similar trend. It has been observed that specialised aurochs hunting was characteristic of the second part of the Neolithic in Hungary. The remains of this large ruminant, as well as those of the most frequently hunted species such as red deer and wild boar, tend to exceed the statistically expected numbers in Late Neolithic deposits. Nevertheless, data from 12 Late Neolithic sites showed that animal husbandry was as important as hunting in this period as well. The number of mammalian species kept and hunted at the various sites was determined mainly by the environmental possibilities, but was also strongly influenced by the mental attitudes of the people at the beginning and the end of the Neolithic (BARTOSIEWICZ 2005).

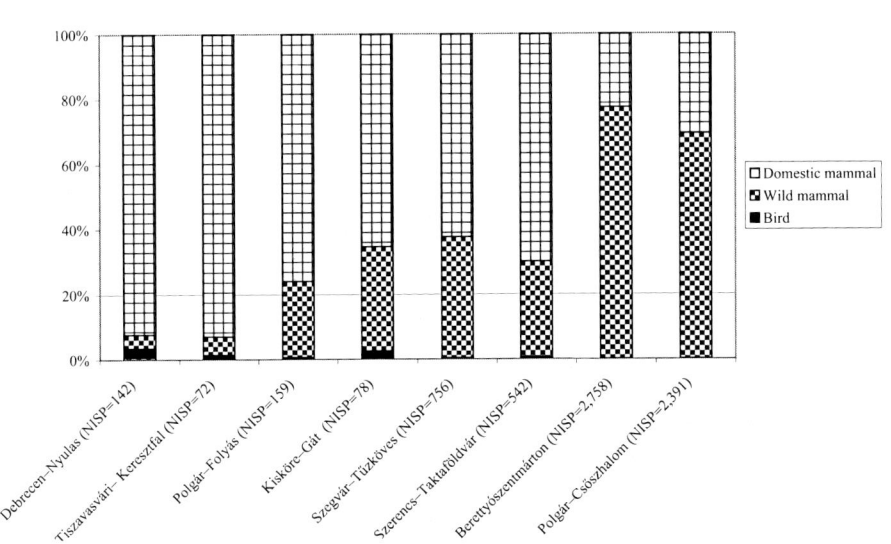

Fig. 10. Percentual distributions of the number of identifiable specimens (NISP) of the main animal groups at Middle Neolithic sites in the Great Hungarian Plain.

6. Bird Remains from Chalcolithic Sites in Hungary

6.1 Tiszapolgár culture sites

Kisköre–Szingegát (Heves County)

The 325 m² site, located on a levee, elevating from the former flood plain of the Tisza, was excavated by Pál Patay in 1966 (PATAY 1966). Three bones of a white-tailed eagle were found in Pit a_1, which were later identified by Dénes Jánossy (JÁNOSSY 1985: 70).

Mezőzombor–Községi temető (Borsod-Abaúj-Zemplén County)

The multi-period site is located on a hillock in the yet unused section of the cemetery of the village of Mezőzombor. In addition to Neolithic and Bronze Age graves, pits from Neolithic, Chalcolithic, Bronze Age and Roman Period settlements were excavated (CSENGERI – PATAY 2002). It is the northernmost Chalcolithic site of this study (*Fig. 1*). The avian remains examined in this work originate from the rescue excavation of 2001, under the direction of Piroska Csengeri and Róbert Patay, succeeding the rescue excavation carried out by Judit Koós and Nándor Kalicz in 2000. The non-avian animal bones were identified by Márta Daróczi-Szabó. Only eight bird remains were found in the assemblage, yielding the following taxa: unidentifiable large wading bird, grey-lag goose, mallard, unidentifiable diurnal bird of prey and coot.

6.2 Sites of the Tiszapolgár–Bodrogkeresztúr transition period

Tiszavalk–Tetes (Borsod-Abaúj-Zemplén County)

The site is located at the northern edge of the village of Tiszavalk on the western bank of the Tetes brooklet. A test excavation was carried out here by Pál Patay in 1968, followed by systematic excavations between 1973 and 1975 (PATAY 1969; PATAY 1971: 9–10). An area of 639 m² was unearthed at this site; a settlement and a cemetery with 25 graves were discovered (PATAY 1978; PATAY 1987). The non-avian bone remains were identified by István Vörös. The only bird bone of the site was found during the 1968 test excavation, in the first of the two pits that were recognized as belonging to the Chalcolithic (VÖRÖS 1986b: 89, Table 5). It was identified by Dénes Jánossy (JÁNOSSY 1985: 75) as belonging to a spoonbill.

6.3 Hunyadihalom culture sites

Tiszalúc–Sarkad (Borsod-Abaúj-Zemplén County)

The settlement is located at the western edge of the village of Tiszalúc, on the right bank of the Sarkad brooklet, 600 m from the former floodplain of the Tisza river. It was discovered by Nándor Kalicz in 1960 and excavated by Pál Patay in 1974. Several houses and almost 200 pits and pit-complexes were uncovered at this site extending over 6868 m^2 (PATAY 1987). The numerous domestic features contained outstanding quantities of animal remains, including fish scales, mussel shell and bones. The majority of the latter belonged to domestic mammals, but several special wild animals such as elk (*Alces alces* Linnaeus 1758), fallow-deer (*Dama mesopotamica* Brooke 1875) and Persian lion (*Panthera leo persica* Meyer 1826) were identified among the hunted mammals (VÖRÖS 1987). Eleven avian remains were also brought to light. They belonged to the following seven taxa: great crested grebe, spoonbill, whooper swan, unidentifiable duck species, golden eagle, white-tailed eagle and crane (JÁNOSSY 1985: 74).

6.4 Discussion

The Chalcolithic is the most poorly represented prehistoric period in this study of avian remains from the Great Hungarian Plain (GÁL 2004; GÁL 2007c). In addition to the sites presented in this work, however, some multi-period settlements from the region of Lake Balaton yielded Chalcolithic avian bones (GÁL 2007a).

Data on fowling are available from four Chalcolithic settlements in the Great Hungarian Plain. Three of these (Kisköre–Szingegát, Mezőzombor–Temető and Tiszavalk–Tetes) belong to the Tiszapolgár culture in the Early Chalcolithic, while the settlement of Tiszaluc–Sarkad represents the Hunyadihalom culture dated to the end of the Middle Chalcolithic.

Compared with the sites of Tiszavalk–Tetes and Kisköre–Szingegát which yielded only one to three remains from one species and one individual each, Mezőzombor–Temető and Tiszalúc–Sarkad offered a greater number of both bone remains and taxa. Species living in or close to wetlands, as well as diurnal birds of prey preferring woodland habitats, are characteristic of Tiszalúc–Sarkad. However, crane and steppe species also occurred here (*Table 9*).

Twelve bird taxa have been identified from this period: ten to the level of species, one to the level of genus and one to the level of family. Similarly to the representation of ecotypes during the Neolithic, almost half (5) of the species are

Table 9. List of bird taxa identified from Chalcolithic sites in Hungary (NISP/MNI).

Taxon		Habitat	Seasonality	Food	Early Chalcolithic			Middle Chalcolithic		Late Chalcolithic	
					Tiszapolgár			Tiszapolgár–Bodrogkeresztúr		Hunyadihalom	
					Kisköre–Szingegát	Mezőzombor–Községi temető		Tiszavalk–Tetes			Tiszalúc–Sarkad
Podiceps cristatus	Great crested grebe	A	SV/R	C						1	
Platalea leucorodia	Spoonbill	A	SV	C				1		1	
Ciconiiformes indet.	unidentifiable wading bird					1					1
Cygnus cygnus	Whooper swan	A	SV/WV	H							
Anser anser	Grey-lag goose	S	SV	H		1					
Anas platyrhynchos	Mallard	A	SV/R	O		2/1					
Anas sp.	unidentifiable duck	A								1	
Haliaeetus albicilla	White-tailed eagle	GF	R	C	3/1					5/2	
Accipiter gentilis	Goshawk	W	R	C		1					
Aquila chrysaetos	Golden eagle	W	R	C/S						1	
Fulica atra	Coot	A	SV/R	C		1					
Grus grus	Crane	S	SV/P	C						1	
Aves indet.	unidentifiable bird					2					
Total					3/1	8/5		1		11/8	

aquatic birds, many are characteristic of gallery forests. Grey-lag goose and crane are the only steppe birds, while goshawk and golden eagle represent woodland habitats. Spoonbill, the only wading bird identified to the level of species, and the white-tailed eagle have been described in the material from two sites each. The rest of the species occurred at individual Chalcolithic sites.

Most of the identified birds are summer visitors. Some of them, such as the great crested grebe, the mallard and the coot, over-winter in the region when the cold season is mild. Resident species are only represented by three diurnal birds of prey (white-tailed eagle, goshawk and golden eagle).

The non-avian bone remains identified from Chalcolithic settlements in the Great Hungarian plain clearly show that livestock farming formed the basis of meat provisioning (VÖRÖS 1983; VÖRÖS 1986b; VÖRÖS 1987). Usually, cattle keeping was characteristic of these societies, but the remains of Caprinae dominated bone assemblages at some sites such as Gyöngyöshalász–Encspuszta at the foot of the Mátra Hills. The greater number of bones from small ruminants was especially noted in deposits indicative of sacrificial contexts, such as the cemeteries at Tiszapolgár–Basatanya and Tiszavalk–Tetes (VÖRÖS 1986b: 88, Table 4).

As evidenced by the quantities of shell, fish and bone remains from wild animals and the great variety of species, fishing and hunting were important activities during the Chalcolithic as well. Nevertheless, the exploitation of these natural resources did not play such an important role in the life of people as in the previous period, that is, in the Middle Neolithic and Late Neolithic. This trend is clearly reflected in large deposits of great representative value, such as the Hunyadihalom culture site of Tiszalúc–Sarkad, although the other two sites discussed in this chapter also confirm the same tendency (*Fig. 11*).

Similarly to the Neolithic and Chalcolithic bone assemblages excavated from South-East Romania, the evidence of fowling was compared to the hunting of wild mammals in the Great Hungarian Plain. *Figure 12*, concentrating on the results obtained from the largest Early Neolithic (Körös culture) materials, shows a similar trend to the graph shown in *Figure 6*, the summary of Gumelniţa culture assemblages. Taxonomic richness, that is, the number of identified species, was more closely connected with assemblage size in the case of the avian material than that of wild mammals. A greater variety of birds were exploited in this case as well. The slightly lower correlations in *Figure 12* in comparison to *Figure 6*, though still statistically significant ($P \leq 0.005$) for both vertebrate classes, is probably due to the smaller number of Early Neolithic sites (7) used in the calculation.

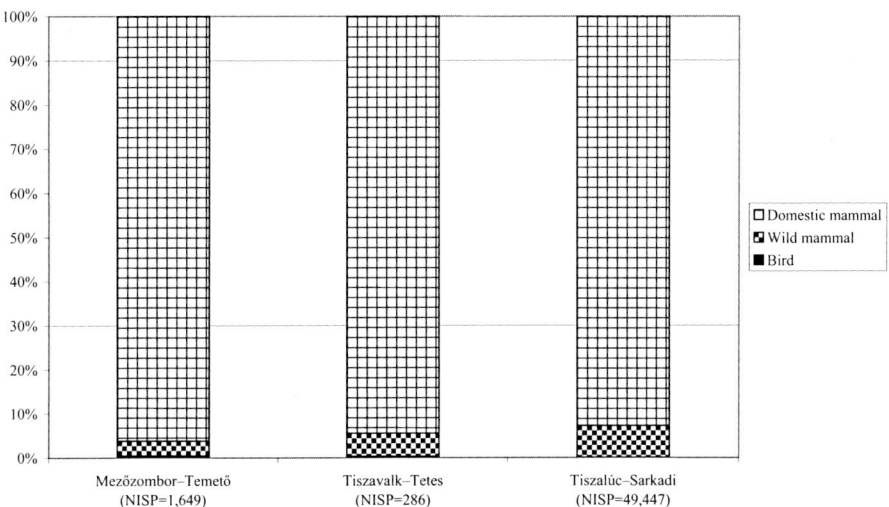

Fig. 11. Percentual distributions of the number of identifiable specimens (NISP) of the main animal groups at Chalcolithic sites in the Great Hungarian Plain.

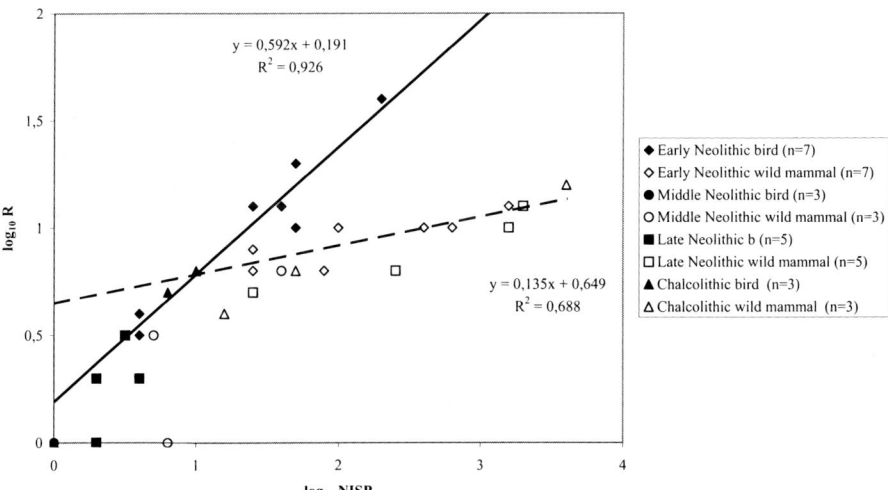

Fig. 12. Relationship between the number of identifiable specimens (NISP, x) and the number of species identified (R, y) in Neolithic and Chalcolithic bone assemblages from the Great Hungarian Plain. Continuous trend line: Early Neolithic birds; dashed trend line: Early Neolithic mammals.

7. Taphonomic Observations on the Assemblages and Individual Remains

The avian remains discussed in this work may be grouped into two major categories. Bird bones identified by previous specialists in recent decades form the first group. These assemblages were not available to me and thus I could rely only on published data. Nevertheless, these works have proven useful since all the bird bones – both complete and fragmented – have been itemized in them (BÖKÖNYI – JÁNOSSY 1965; JÁNOSSY 1985).

The assemblages analysed by myself form the second, larger group, which includes all the remains excavated from South-East Romania, as well as five Neolithic and one Copper Age assemblages from the Great Hungarian Plain. These materials, especially the larger ones, provided first-hand data on the probable exploitation of certain birds. Consequently, the following chapters will be based upon mainly my personal observations regarding the frequency of bones and noted interventions.

There are four major phases within the taphonomic process, that is, the *post mortem* history of animal remains. Biostratonomy refers to all effects prior to deposition, including intentional, primary human action, such as butchery, transport and cooking, as well as natural damage (e.g. weathering and animal gnawing). The next phase, fossil diagenesis, is the result of natural (physical, chemical, biological, etc.) processes that act selectively on the remains after deposition. During this second stage, secondary human action (e.g. ploughing) may cause disturbances in the deposit in subsequent periods, damaging the archaeological record. The last two phases, field surveys/excavations and the documentation and study of remains (referred to at the beginning of this chapter), also influence the obtained results, sometimes in a most subjective manner (O'CONNOR 2000: 21; BARTOSIEWICZ 2001: 83, Table 3).

The avian assemblages studied in this work come from a number of excavations carried out within a time span of approximately 40 years, at which I did not have the opportunity to participate, but I have been given access to the bird bones that were distinguished. Therefore I have mostly been able to make notes concerning the biostratonomy of the remains in the absence of first-hand information on the soil matrix. Thus the studied remains offer information on the cultural context of avian finds rather than on the taphonomic process as a whole. Coincidentally, archaeologists are most likely to be interested in the following biostratonomic implications of avian assemblages.

7.1 Depositional features

According to the descriptions in archaeological reports, the bird bone assemblages derived from domestic features, such as dwellings and refuse pits. Therefore, we may consider these remains the end-product of certain human activities. In the case of the three well-represented assemblages brought to light at South-East Romanian tell settlements, under continuous excavation for a longer period, a number of bird remains originated from well-defined archaeological contexts.

87 avian bones representing 14 taxa were found in a total of 15 house complexes at Hârșova. Most of the identified species were waterfowl. Remains from medium- and large-sized birds with tasty meat, such as swan, goose and duck, are especially frequent. Smaller and larger wading birds, diurnal birds of prey and song birds were also identified. Context 521 stands out among the other features by the high number of specimens and species identified. The water-sieving of over 7.6 kg of coprolites from this feature offered an opportunity to study the seasonal deposition of remains. The spores and pollens that were obtained indicated that part of the domestic residue had deposited from late spring to autumn, while the other part from the late autumn to early spring (CIMEC 1998). Most of the avian remains from this feature suggest the storage and exploitation of complete birds. Juvenile and subadult specimens indicative of spring and summer fowling were recognized as well (*Table 6*).

Two houses, ten complexes and three pits yielded altogether 81 bird bones representing 13 taxa at Borduşani Popină. House SL 43, which contained the remains of the left wing from a glossy ibis and one bone from a mallard and a crow each, had been abandoned in several stages. Eight accumulations including ash, potsherd, bone tools and charcoal were discovered among the remains of the collapsed walls. It has been presumed that these deposits result from well defined activities (CIMEC 2004b). The skeleton of a white egret was found in Context 46. The (mostly wing) remains of other large wading birds, such as grey- and purple heron, stork and glossy ibis, were also identified from the aforementioned features. The booted eagle, yielding a complete carpometacarpus, is the only diurnal bird of prey identified from the building complexes. One of the three pits (Trench J4) contained the skeleton of a mallard and a bone from a magpie. Abundant material from the second pit included the skeletal parts of grey heron, mallard, coot, three crows and magpie. The third pit yielded a single bone from a grey-lag goose (*Table 5*).

Five avian remains have been identified from three houses at the third best-represented Gumelniţa culture site in this region, the Vităneşti tell. An incomplete coracoideum from a crane was found in House 1 that measured 4 by 4 m. This building was equipped with two fireplaces, one inside and the other outside of the house (CIMEC 1996). House 2 (measuring 5 by 4 m) yielded a tibiotarsus fragment from a crane as well as a coracoideum fragment from a male great bustard. Three clay weights and several antler artefacts were found in this dwelling. A sternum fragment from a female great bustard, as well as a tibiotarsus fragment from a medium-sized bird, was identified from House 5 (6 by 4 m). Numerous isolated accumulations of potsherds were also found in this feature. House 5 was destroyed by a heavy fire (CIMEC 1997b).

7.2 Modifications on individual bones

Contemporaneous modifications observed on bones may be grouped into three categories: cut marks, traces of burning and gnawing marks. Considering the first category, I have noted cut marks that evidence the butchery or defleshing on the one hand, and some that may be related to meat consumption on the other hand. Most of the cut marks were made during the processing of the quarry. Such marks may be seen on two bones from a grey-lag goose, for example. Both the single cut mark on the coracoideum excavated from Căscioarele and on the carpometacarpus (*Plate 1*, *Fig. 1–2*) found at Borduşani–Popină suggest that they were inflicted when the bird had already been chopped into pieces. The latter bone has a brownish colour that is suggestive of burning as well. Considering the location and depth of the cut mark noted on the carpometacarpus from a whooper swan (Hârşova), probably it was also made when dismembering the bones of the wing.

Numerous cut marks were observed on the two sides of the distal part of a crane tibiotarsus from Grădiştea–Coslogeni. The fine and careful marks were most probably also aimed at the cautious detachment of the tibiotarsus from the tarsometatarsus (*Plate 1*, *Fig. 3*). Since the tibiotarsus does not show further marks of human activity, it is likely that the tarsometatarsus was utilized in some way. Although no prehistoric evidence is known so far, the tarsometatarsi of the crane were a popular raw material during the Avar Period (AD 6th–8th c.) in the Carpathian Basin. Owing to their long, regular shape and square cross-sections,

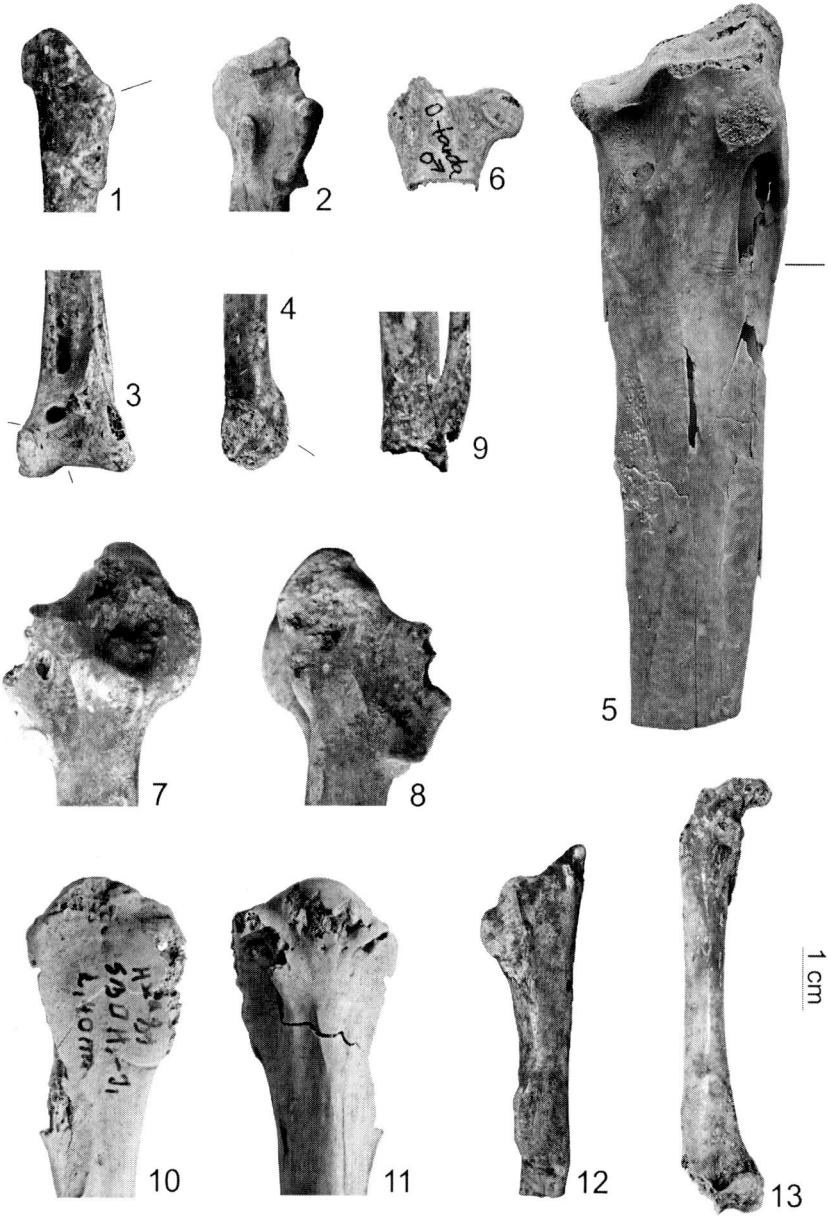

Plate 1. Marks of cutting, gnawing and pathological lesions.

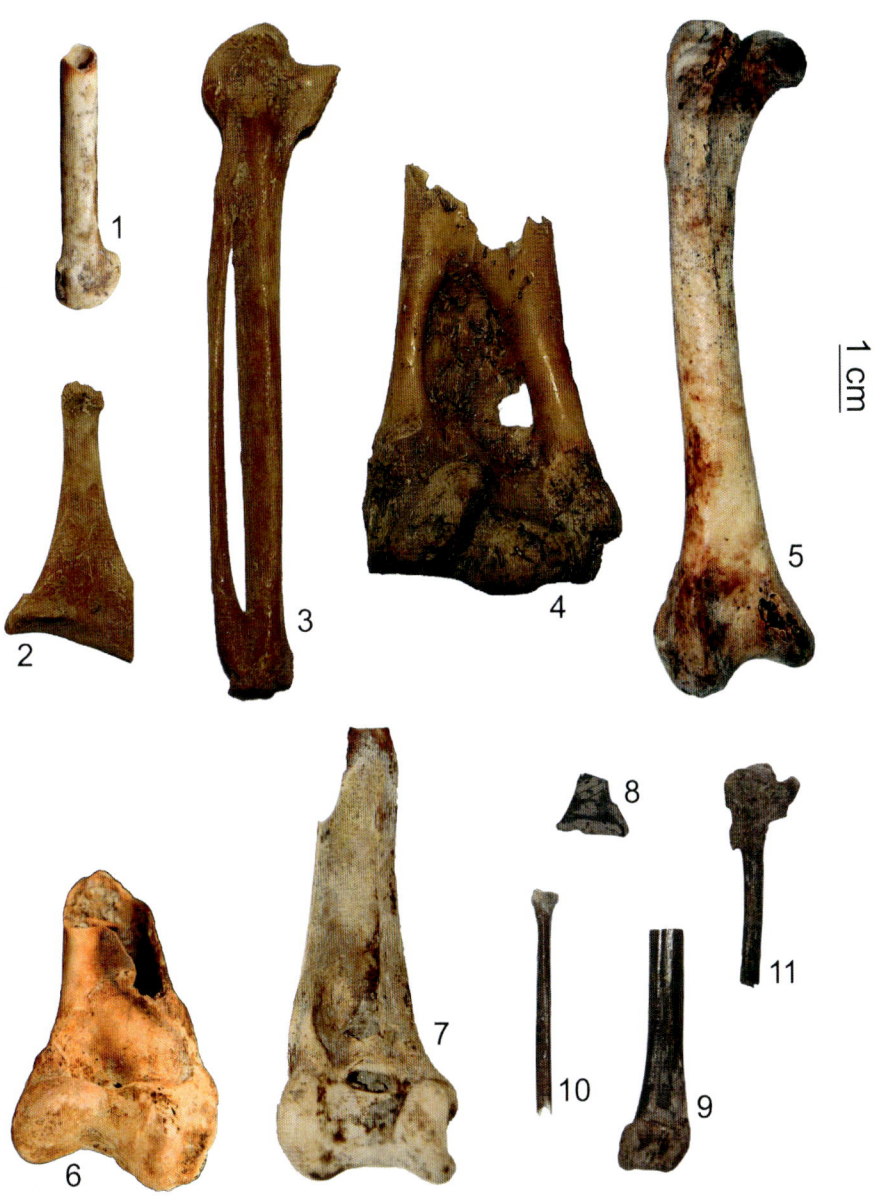

Plate 2. Traces of burning.

these bones were often carved into single or double pipes (KOZÁK 1997; GÁL 2006b).

The distal fragment of an ulna from a lesser spotted eagle, found at Căscioarele, showed an incision that may also have been caused during the dismemberment of wing bones (*Plate 1, Fig. 4*). Finally, blanks found at two Gumelnița culture sites indicate that avian bones were also considered an important raw material in the Chalcolithic of South-East Romania. In addition to the various raw materials of animal origins, such as antler, mammalian bones, teeth and shells found in Bordușani–Popină (VOINEA 1997), two bird bones showing cut marks indicative of manufacturing were found at other two contemporaneous sites. The ulna fragment of a white pelican from Însurăței displayed the beginnings of working on two sections of the diaphysis (*Plate 1, Fig. 5*).

The long and straight cut mark seen on the proximal fragment of a femur from a great bustard (Vitănești) also suggests that the diaphysis of the bone was probably utilized (*Plate 1, Fig. 6*). Even though a number of avian bone implements are known from archaeological sites in both Romania and Hungary, none of them were made from the femur (GÁL 2005). This skeletal part is usually short and fragile in birds, since the wall of the bone is especially thin. Fragility, as a consequence of the thin bone, is also characteristic of the ulna of the pelican. It is somehow strange, therefore, that both blanks found in the rather large Gumelnița bird bone samples were made from unsuitable skeletal parts. Since these artefacts were either never finished or abandoned, their function remains uncertain.

Another hint to human activity are the traces of burning observed on skeletal parts. These usually offer evidence for the cooking and roasting of animals. One has to take into consideration, however, that a number of bones may have ended up in or near fireplaces by accident. Also, the burning down of houses at certain settlements may have affected domestic residue, leaving marks of secondary burning on the bones.

Only one Neolithic avian find from Romania showed traces of burning. This is the distal fragment of an ulna from a tawny owl, found in Context 854 at Măgura–Buduiasca. Since only the diaphysis was affected (*Plate 2, Fig. 1*), it is very likely that the bone was broken under the effect of heat. Since no archaeological evidence suggests the consumption of meat from owls, the bone was most probably part of a utensil or some decoration, burnt during a ritual or simply by accident.

Gumelnița culture avian finds are more numerous from the Romanian deposits and most of them seem to be simple food refuse. The tell site of Bordușani Popină yielded eight burnt bones. The most spectacular of them occurred on the almost complete coracoideum from a ferruginous duck, the complete carpometacarpus from a grey-lag goose and the distal fragment of a humerus from a great bustard (*Plate 2, Fig. 2–4*).

The Hârșova tell settlement also yielded four burnt bones. In addition to the complete femur from a grey-lag goose, distal fragments of a femur and a tibiotarsus from a whooper swan showed similar traces (*Plate 2, Fig. 5–7*). Carbonized bones of a diurnal bird of prey (Accipitriformes sp. indet.) and of a small song bird (Passeriformes sp. indet.) were found in Complex 644 and Complex 521, respectively. A couple of burnt bones were found at the rest of the Chalcolithic sites: a humerus fragment from a cormorant at the Luncavița tell, as well as a coracoideum and a humerus fragment from a black grouse at the Vitănești tell.

In Hungary, only two Körös culture settlements yielded burnt bones among the assemblages studied by myself. The settlement of Ecsegfalva 23 provided charred bones from gadwall (coracoideum), mallard (tibiotarsus) and another duck (coracoideum). Fragments of carbonized skeletal parts from teal (coracoideum), goosander (tibiotarsus), coot (radius) and woodpigeon (carpometacarpus) were also found (*Plate 2, Fig. 8–11*). The site of Nagykörű–Tsz. yielded burnt bones from grey-lag goose (humerus), mallard (ulna) and pochard (tibiotarsus).

The third category of bone modifications, gnawing marks, are more difficult to interpret than cut marks and traces of burning, because they may have been caused by people and animals alike. Considering the second group, carnivorous and omnivorous species, such as dog, cat and pig, should be considered above all, but we should not exclude the possibility that some wild animals also had access to the discarded food remains. Although distinctions between taxonomic groups on the basis of gnawing marks left on animal bones were made in a number of recent and palaeontological assemblages (LYMAN 1994: 205–216), conducting similar studies concerning bird remains is almost impossible. According to the observations made on fresh bone remains, adult dogs and pigs tend to chew up these usually small and fragile bones completely. Other experiments suggested that even kittens can consume the long bones of juvenile chickens in whole and adult cats are able to consume complete chicken carcasses (STALLIBRASS 1990: 158). In the case of archaeological remains, the examples below suggest that often only the epiphyseal ends – usually holding remains of flesh, cartilage, tendons, etc. after human discard – were gnawed and eaten, which would be more characteristic of puppies and scavengers with relatively weaker teeth, such as felids (N.B. domestic cats should not be reckoned within the prehistoric periods under discussion).

Evidence of such partially eaten bones was found at the Criş culture site of Măgura–Buduiasca, as well as the Gumelniţa culture tell settlements of Borduşani Popină, Căscioarele and Hârşova. Borduşani Popină yielded most of these remains: altogether 11 gnawed bones. Five such bones were found at Hârşova. The carpometacarpus from a whooper swan was complete but damaged by punctures on both ends (*Plate 1, Fig. 7–9*). Similar traces were observed on the proximal humerus fragment from a white-tailed eagle found at Căscioarele (*Plate 1, Fig. 10–11*). Although, as mentioned before, gnawing marks cannot be exclusively attributed to dogs, it is worth mentioning that dog remains were rather frequent at the sites mentioned: 1343=14.4% of NISP at Borduşani Popină, 896=16.9% at Hârşova and 22=13.0% at Căscioarele (BĂLĂŞESCU *et al.* 2005: 203–206, Table 7–10).

I have identified only one gnawed bird bone from among the bone assemblages from Hungary, coming from the Körös culture site of Nagykörű Tsz, where six dog remains (1.3% of NISP) were also identified (RACZKY *et al.* 2007).

7.3 The anatomical distribution of bones

In addition to direct interventions reflected on the remains themselves, indirect information pointing to the possible exploitation of animals may also be gained from the analysis of the assemblages as a whole. Bone frequencies and species representation were considered in the largest assemblages recovered by water-sieving, offering the possibly most complete representation of avian remains.

One may note in *Figure 13* that generally wing bones dominated in these assemblages. The most frequent among them is the humerus, which bears significant quantities of meat by its own musculature and as part of the shoulder girdle as well. Nevertheless, the abundance of bones from the distal part of the wing with a low nutritive value hint to alternative uses of wings as well.

The small number of *phalanges anteriores* compared to the long bones of the wing is also striking. The selective transport of body parts (e.g. the discarding of the head, the wing tips and legs at the place of hunting) to the settlement, pre-depositional loss (owing to the access of dogs to household refuse), as well as sampling and identification bias (e.g. the loss or misidentification of these bones) all may have contributed to the under-representation of these small and not easily recognizable skeletal parts. Nevertheless, they were especially frequent at the

Körös culture site of Ecsegfalva 23, which offered a special interpretation for the possible exploitation of birds at this settlement (see below).

The second best-represented skeletal parts following the humerus were the tibiotarsus and coracoideum. These bones are also richly covered in flesh and were thus preferred from the viewpoint of meat procurement. Owing to their compact structures, they also have a better chance for surviving different taphonomic agents.

The other skeletal parts are rather under-represented. The scarcity of remains from particularly fragile bones, such as the skull, the sternum, the pelvis and the small vertebrae and phalanges is a general characteristic of avian assemblages. Due to their osteological structures and/or sizes, these bones are more prone to damage inflicted during the butchery, cooking and consumption of birds, as well as destruction by pre- and post-depositional taphonomic agents. Nevertheless, the modest representation of the femur as one of the bones with the greatest meat value, or the tarsometatarsus, a rather compact skeletal part, is rather surprising at a number of sites. The delicate structure of the femur might offer an explanation for the first trend. The selective transport of body parts (i.e. early discard of meatless feet) may sometimes explain the lack of tarsometatarsi. The number of these bones, however, considerably varied between the sites studied.

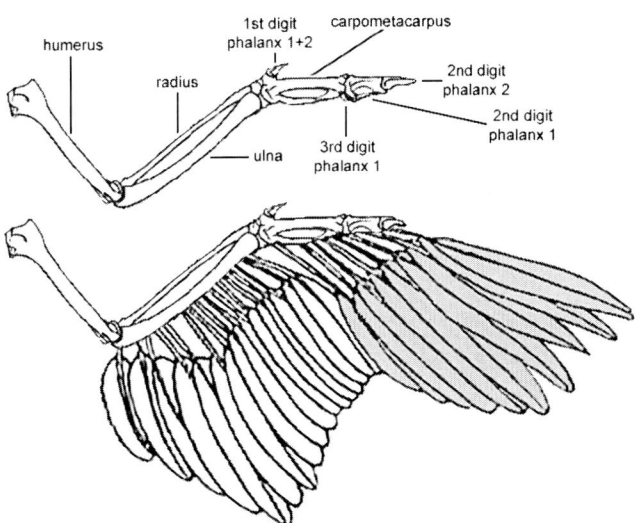

Fig. 13. Bones of the bird wing and the position of main feathers. Primary remiges are marked by shading (drawn by László Bartosiewicz).

It is worth mentioning that only one of the hand-collected assemblages, Endrőd 3/6, showed anatomical distribution of bones similar to those of the aforementioned cases. Wing bones (including the most frequent humeri: 36 specimens providing 28%) clearly dominated by 49% among the remains. In this assemblage the femur followed the coracoideum, however, there was no considerable difference between the number of femora and tibiotarsi.

Beyond the general observations concerning the distribution of bones, which reflect some of the features of individual bones on a larger scale, the detailed analysis of each assemblage is the key to finding characteristic differences between the hunting and use of birds at the studied settlements.

One may note that phalanges from the wing and carpometacarpi – which together form the tip of the wing – were rather frequent at the Körös culture site of Ecsegfalva 23 in the Great Hungarian Plain. Seventy-one per cent of the skeletal parts from woodpigeon represented the tip of the wing, but large wading birds also provided a number of these skeletal parts. It is well-known that the middle part and especially the distal end of the wing are very poor in meat, which renders it useless from a nutritional point of view. However, the largest feathers, the primary remiges, are attached to the carpometacarpus and the phalanges (*Fig. 13*).

Since there is plenty of ethnographic and historic evidence for the use of the tip of the wing with the feathers attached, it has been hypothesised that people settled at Ecsegfalva made use of objects that included these bones. It was also observed in this assemblage that cranial remains were entirely missing and only a few vertebrae were found in spite of water-sieving. An optional explanation would be the fragility and small size of these bones, but other delicate or tiny skeletal parts, such as the fragile sternum, the clavicula, the anterior phalanges, etc. were also collected. Meanwhile, leg bones were under-represented as well. I have therefore interpreted the complete absence of skulls and the small number of bones from the foot with the removal of head and lower legs in most cases, and the selective transport of bird bodies to the settlement (GÁL 2007b). Nevertheless, the consumption of brain as a delicacy may also have motivated the smashing of skulls of larger birds.

The two most abundant Chalcolithic assemblages from South-East Romania, Hârşova and Borduşani–Popină, showed other features. The bones from both the head and neck, as well as the foot, were found in relatively great numbers at these sites. At Hârşova the frequency of phalanges from the foot is noteworthy (*Fig. 14*), indicating that complete birds had been brought to the tell settlements.

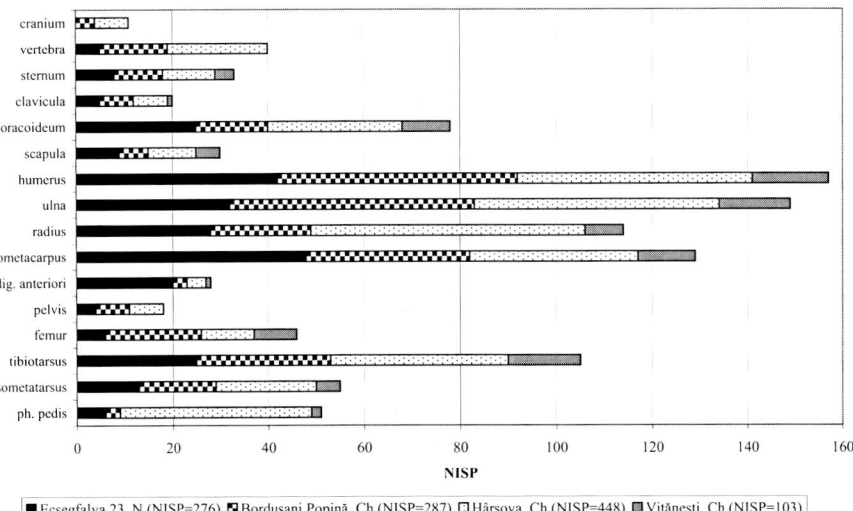

Fig. 14. Distribution of skeletal parts at the most abundant (n>103) Neolithic and Chalcolithic sites. Abbreviations: N – Neolithic; Ch – Chalcolithic.

The complete skeleton of a mallard found in the pit in Trench J4 at Borduşani–Popină (*Table 5*), remains from grey heron, glossy ibis, grey-lag goose, moorhen and crow in Complex 521 at Hârşova, as well as the sternum and shoulder bones of a white-tailed eagle at both sites and two other eagle species at Hârşova (*Table 10*) offer evidence supporting this idea. In spite of the poorer material from Vitănești, where the remains were hand-collected, one may conclude from the anatomical representation of bones that at least some species, such as the black grouse, the crane and the great bustard were transported to the habitation without previous dismemberment.

7.4 Discussion

The avian bones presented in this study display a number of features both directly and indirectly. Many of these are often related to each other. It is evident from the nature of the identified bird taxa (*Table 3–4* and *Table 7–9*), as well as the traces of butchery, burning and gnawing, that most of the hunted birds were eaten. This idea is also evidenced by the frequency of identifiable remains originating from a number of species. Bones of the grey-lag goose (whose domesticated form is still exploited for its meat, egg and down), were especially numerous at Hârşova,

Table 10. *Birds of prey and their skeletal parts identified from South-East Romania (bold case letters indicate the tip of the wing and phalanges). Abbreviations: N – Neolithic; Ch – Chalcolithic.*

Taxon	Sex	Skeletal part	Fragmentation	Site	Age	Culture
Accipitriformes						
Haliaeetus albicilla		**phalanx anterior 1/II**	proximal fragment	Măgura–Buduiasca	N	Dudeşti
Pernis apivorus		coracoideum	incomplete	Grădiştea–Coslogeni	N	Boian-Bolintineanu
Accipiter gentilis	female	femur	distal fragment	Ciulniţa	N	Boian-Giuleşti
Aquila chrysaetos		phalanx pedis 3/II	complete	Isaccea–Suhat	N	Boian-Giuleşti
Haliaeetus albicilla	male	coracoideum	incomplete	Borduşani–Popină	Ch	Gumelniţa
Haliaeetus albicilla		humerus	distal fragment			
Haliaeetus albicilla	female	**carpometacarpus**	complete			
Haliaeetus albicilla		**carpometacarpus**	proximal fragment			
Haliaeetus albicilla		**phalanx anterior 1/II**	complete			
Haliaeetus albicilla		femur	distal fragment			
Aquila heliaca		femur	proximal fragment			
Hieraaetus pennatus	male	**carpometacarpus**	complete			
Haliaeetus albicilla	male	**carpometacarpus**	complete	Căscioarele	Ch	Gumelniţa
Aquila pomarina		ulna	distal fragment			
Hieraaetos pennatus		ulna	distal fragment			
Pernis apivorus	male	radius	complete	Hârşova	Ch	Gumelniţa
Haliaeetus albicilla		sternum	fragment			
Haliaeetus albicilla		scapula				
Haliaeetus albicilla		humerus	proximal fragment			
Haliaeetus albicilla		humerus	distal fragment			
Haliaeetus albicilla		radius	diaphysis			

Taxon	Sex	Skeletal part	Fragmentation	Site	Age	Culture
Haliaeetus albicilla	male	ulna	proximal fragment			
Haliaeetus albicilla		**carpometacarpus**	distal fragment			
Haliaeetus albicilla		phalanx pedis	incomplete			
Haliaeetus albicilla		phalanx pedis (toe)	complete			
Accipiter gentilis	male	humerus	distal fragment			
Accipiter gentilis	male	ulna	complete			
Buteo buteo	male	**carpometacarpus**	incomplete			
Buteo buteo	male	**carpometacarpus**	complete			
Aquila pomarina		coracoideum	incomplete			
Aquila cf. clanga		**carpometacarpus**	complete			
Aquila chrysaetos		coracoideum	diaphysis			
Aquila chrysaetos		radius	diaphysis			
Aquila sp.		radius	diaphysis			
Hieraetus pennatus	male	**carpometacarpus**	complete			
Pandion haliaetus	female	tarsometatarsus	distal fragment			
Accipitriformes indet.		radius	distal fragment			
Accipitriformes indet.		phalanx pedis	distal			
Accipitriformes indet.		phalanx pedis (toe)	complete			
Haliaeetus albicilla	female	humerus	distal fragment	Insurăței	Ch	Gumelnița
Accipiter gentilis	male	ulna	proximal fragment	Luncavița	Ch	Gumelnița
Gypaetus barbatus		**carpometacarpus**	incomplete	Vitănești	Ch	Gumelnița
Circus macrourus		**carpometacarpus**	proximal fragment			
Falco peregrinus	male	femur	incomplete			
Strigiformes						
Strix aluco		ulna	distal fragment	Măgura–Buduiasca	N	Starčevo-Criș
Strix aluco		humerus	proximal fragment	Vitănești	Ch	Gumelnița
Asio flammeus		tarsometatars	distal fragment			

and well represented at Borduşani–Popină. The swan was also a preferred fowl at these sites. Mallard dominated Borduşani–Popină, Endrőd 3/6 and Ecsegfalva 23; ferruginous duck was also frequent at the latter site. In addition to ducks, coot was often chosen among aquatic birds at Ecsegfalva 23 and Borduşani–Popină. Black grouse and great bustard, these medium and large-sized tasty birds were the most hunted species at Vitănești (*Fig. 15*). Although represented by a smaller number of remains, the rest of the geese and ducks, as well as the partridge, the spotted crake, the moorhen, the crane and the little bustard may be surely grouped into the category of birds for consumption.

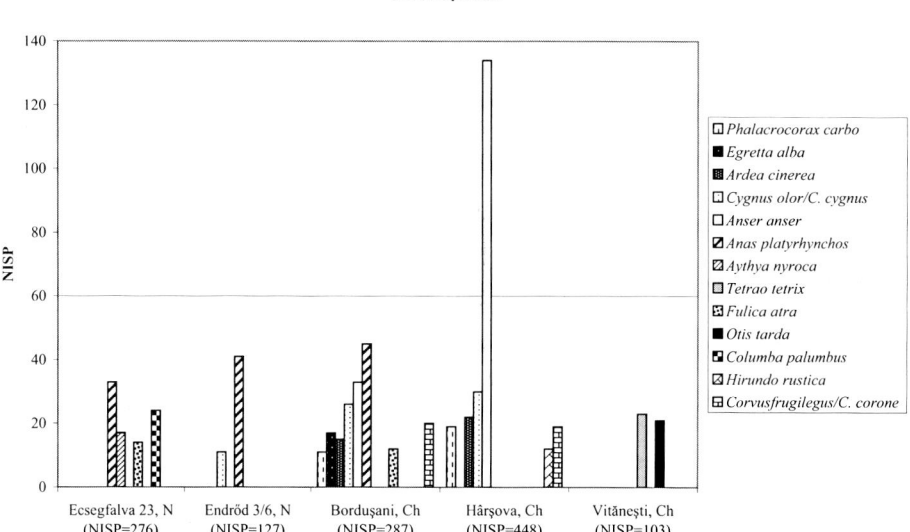

Fig. 15. Bone frequencies of the most common species (n<10) identified from the largest assemblages. Abbreviations: N – Neolithic; Ch – Chalcolithic.

Even if the meat of a number of species, such as the cormorant and large wading birds, which mainly feed on fish, is considered inedible by modern taste (one of the Hungarian popular names for the cormorant is "smelly bird"), we may not exclude them from the diet of ancient peoples. Cormorants are feared and rigorously chased by fishermen, as these gluttonous birds represent a great competition in fishing. An adult cormorant needs c.a. 3 kg of fish per day; they live in stocks and usually breed twice a year (CHERNEL 2003). However, if they had been killed by the ancient people only to protect the fishing area, their bodies would not have been carried to the settlement. The frequency, the represented skeletal parts and the bones of young individuals identified from these fowl are all indicative, though indirectly, of the consumption of their meat.

The relatively great number of remains from crows also raises the question of their exploitation. Both rook and hooded crow have become characteristic of human environments in the past centuries, but these birds are originally found in forest-steppe habitats. They often accompany the stocks of herons and cormorants in gallery forests. Crows are omnivorous, eating food of vegetal and animal origins alike. Scavenging is also characteristic of these birds. Written sources offer evidence of the consumption of crows at the end of the 17th century (BENDA – VÁRKONYI 2001: 274). The recipes from that time suggested their preparation similarly to that of other fowl, namely cooking them in their own blood. The liquid thus obtained was seasoned by different spices and herbs, and termed "black juice" (BENDA 2004). According to the ethnographic record, crows were trapped by snaring and eaten in South-Western Hungary during the 20th century (KARDOS 1943: 19).

The great variety of diurnal birds of prey in both studied regions, as well as their possible forms of exploitation offered another subject of investigation. Twelve and six species were identified from South-East Romania (*Table 10*) and the Great Hungarian Plain (*Table 11*), respectively. Almost every site yielded at least one bone from these raptors. Birds ranging from the size of the harrier and the goshawk to that of vultures were recognized, but eagles were the best-represented group. The white-tailed eagle was the most frequently identified diurnal bird of prey; it was recognized from both countries, from the Neolithic and Copper Age alike. This large raptor is characteristic of wetland environments, the habitat type best-represented by the other identified bird species: the white-tailed eagle nests in gallery forests and hunts along fresh waters (PETERSON *et al.* 1977).

Birds of prey feed on living animals and carcasses. Their meat is therefore usually considered inedible and excluded from the human diet. Nevertheless, a German cook book written in the 16th century and translated into Hungarian in 1680 mentions no fewer than nine recipes for the preparation of eagle (LAKÓ 1983: 134). Evidence of butchering and cooking recovered at prehistoric sites from Italy to northern Europe show that birds now regarded "tasteless" or inedible were regularly eaten in the past (CASSOLI – TAGLIACOZZO 1997; MANNERMAA 2003: 19). Bone remains from the fish-eating fulmar (*Fulmarus glacialis*) and great shearwater (*Puffinus gravis*) strongly suggested that these birds were exploited for their meat and oil. Meat from young cormorants was considered a

Table 11. Birds of prey and their skeletal parts identified from the
Great Hungarian Plain (bold case letters indicate the tip of the wing and phalanges).
Abbreviations: N – Neolithic; Ch – Chalcolithic.

Taxon	Sex	Skeletal part	Completeness	Site	Age	Culture
Accipitriformes						
Circus sp.		radius	distal fragment	Ecsegfalva 23	N	Körös
Buteo buteo	male	tarsometatarsus	proximal fragment			
Hieraaetus pennatus	male	tarsometatarsus	proximal fragment			
Haliaeetus albicilla		humerus	proximal fragment	Röszke–Lúdvár	N	Körös
		ulna	complete			
Circaetus gallicus		tibiotarsus	distal fragment			
Circus aeruginosus		femur	complete			
		tibiotarsus	distal fragment			
Haliaeetus albicilla	male	**carpometacarpus**	complete	Szolnok–Szanda	N	Körös
Aquila pomarina	female	tibiotarsus	distal fragment	Tiszaszőlős–Domaháza	N	Körös
Haliaeetus albicilla		**carpometacarpus**	distal fragment	Szegvár–Tűzköves	N	Tisza
Haliaeetus albicilla		ulna	fragment	Szerencs–Taktaföldvár	N	Tisza
Haliaeetus albicilla	male	humerus	distal fragment	Berettyó-szentmárton	N	Herpály
Haliaeetus albicilla		coracoideum	complete	Kisköre–Szingegát	Ch	Tiszapolgár
		scapula	complete			
		humerus	complete			
Accipiter gentilis	male	**carpometacarpus**	complete	Mezőzombor–Községi temető	Ch	Tiszapolgár
Haliaeetus albicilla		ulna	complete	Tiszalúc–Sarkad	Ch	Hunyadihalom
	male	**carpometacarpus**	complete			
	female	**carpometacarpus**	complete			
		carpometacarpus	complete			
		phalanx anterior 1/II	complete			
Strigiformes						
Bubo bubo		tarsometatarsus	distal fragment	Polgár–Csőszhalom	N	Herpály
Strix aluco		**phalanx anterior 1/II**	complete	Ecsegfalva 23	N	Körös
		?	?	Endrőd 119	N	Körös

particular delicacy in Greenland, where ravens were also consumed (GOTFREDSEN – MØBJERG 2004).

Birds of prey, however, were admired and recognized for their special skills, such as their sharp eyesight, feat of flying and hunting skills. Therefore, these birds represented power and probably inspired respect first of all. Ethnographic analogies suggest that their body or displayed feathers may have shown supremacy or forms of status. Similarly to the cormorant, raptors feeding on fish, such as the osprey and the white-tailed eagle, could pose a competition to people during the fishing season. Some of these birds may have been killed as they attacked domestic livestock, especially the young.

Owls, nocturnal birds of prey, were underrepresented in the studied assemblages. A single species, the tawny owl, was identified from the Neolithic in South-East Romania. The Starčevo-Criş culture site of Măgura–Buduiasca yielded the distal fragment of its ulna, which showed traces of burning. The tawny owl (humerus, proximal fragment) and the short-eared eagle (tarsometatarsus, distal fragment) were identified from the Chalcolithic tell site of Vităneşti.

The tawny owl was recognized at two Neolithic settlements in the Great Hungarian Plain as well. The Körös culture site of Ecsegfalva 23 yielded a complete phalanx from the wing, while another remain was found at Endrőd 119. The eagle owl was identified from the Late Neolithic Herpály-Csőszhalom culture: the site of Polgár–Csőszhalom yielded a distal fragment of a tarsometatarsus from this species.

The fear of owls is well-known from written and ethnographic sources. These birds were mostly associated with death and other tragic events such as wars, for example. The symbol of owls or other birds as companions of the soul of the dead goes back to Antiquity. Although only a few remains from owls were identified and none of them were found in house contexts, we may not exclude the role of these birds in ritual activities as early as the Neolithic and Chalcolithic.

The abundance of wing bones was generally characteristic of the avian assemblages under study. In the case of diurnal birds of prey, however, one may observe the frequency of skeletal parts forming the wing tip, just as with the woodpigeon remains in the assemblage of Neolithic Ecsegfalva 23. Almost all carpometacarpi were complete or barely fragmented. Many species were represented only by this single bone. In addition to wing tips, separated feathers must have also been used from the great variety of represented species. Medieval and modern-day customs hint at the appreciation of feathers from large wading birds, diurnal birds of prey, the crane and the great bustard (GÁL, forthcoming a). It is very likely that small and colourful birds, such as the great spotted woodpecker, the roller, the jay (Ecsegfalva 23) and the hoopoe (Borduşani–Popină) were also exploited for their plumage.

The Hunyadihalom culture site of Tiszalúc–Sarkad stands especially out due to the five bones from the white-tailed eagle that represent half of the avian bones that were found. Moreover, a number of tarsometatarsi and phalanges from the foot were also recognized (*Tables 10–11*), which hint at the utilization of feet and toes.

Alhough the abundance of wing bones was observed in a relatively great number of archaeological assemblages and their density was presumed to have been the main natural factor behind this phenomenon, a recent study refutes this hypothesis and indicates that other features, such as selective transport, processing techniques, consumption practices, wing curation and scavenger damage, may all have played a role in producing this pattern (BOVY 2002).

8. Pathological Lesions

In addition to the various types of post-mortem modifications observed on certain finds, two bones identified in the assemblages from South-East Romania showed pathological conditions. Contrary to the taphonomic characteristics of bones, which affect the carcasses and consequently the skeleton after death, these symptoms had developed in the birds and influenced their lives.

It is uncertain whether the two observed traumatic cases had been caused by human activity or natural causes. The scapula fragment from Bevick's swan, found in Complex 756 at the Hârşova tell settlement, showed an outgrowth on the *corpus scapulae*. According to the structure of healing and its location on the lateral surface of the bone, this is probably a callus that developed following a blow (*Plate 1*, *Fig. 12*). It could have been inflicted either by people when attempting to kill the bird on a previous occasion or accidentally, for example, during the long migrations. Species that have to cover long distances between their breeding and wintering areas often get caught in storms or encounter similar kinds of trials.

The second pathological condition was observed on the femur of a male peregrine, recovered from the Vităneşti tell. Since this exostosis appeared on the proximal part of the diaphysis, it is likely that the centre of infection was the pelvic articulation (*Plate 1*, *Fig. 13*). I have found a very similar lesion on the same bone in a young skeleton (nr. 4846) of the same species and sex in the comparative bird bone collection of the Natural History Museum, Vienna. A small degree of shortening in the length of both femora was noted. The bird was kept in captivity by a falconer who attributed the condition to vitamin deficiency (Ernst Bauernfeind, personal communication). According to another hypothesis, the bird would have suffered from gout (Anita Gamauf, personal communication). Whether illness was responsible for the development of the condition, the fact that both bones were affected speaks for a systemic condition. In peregrine, both sexes brood for approximately a month. The male often feeds its pair during hatching (RADU 1983: 139). Therefore, it is hypothesised that this metabolic disorder might have been related to the period of reproduction in spite of the fact that due to its smaller size the bone belonged to a male.

Pathological lesions on avian remains found either in palaeontological or archaeological assemblages are very rare. Usually, only one or two finds surface even in large samples of several hundreds of bones. In spite of their relatively short history, domestic fowl often suffered from different kinds of traumas connected to mass keeping and feeding, such as fractures, rickets and viral illnesses (GÁL forthcoming b). Evidence for pathological conditions in wild birds, on the other hand, is very scarce and their diagnoses and interpretations offer a true challenge to experts.

9. Ornithological Implications

The identification of recently recovered bird bones and a review of the already published data resulted in a summary of avian species hunted over seven to five millennia ago in large areas of present-day Romania and Hungary. Due to the fact that in the past domestic birds were not yet present in Europe and avian meat, egg and feather could be obtained by fowling exclusively, it can be hypothesised that hunted birds give a clear indication of the environmental conditions around the settlements on the one hand, and the composition of the exploited species on the other hand. Such conclusions are even more reliable in the case of those sites where excavation methods included the water-sieving of soil samples and thus the recording of remains from small species may also be expected.

Since the beginning of the Neolithic, increasing sedentism and concomitant population growth required the development of organized social units that included the formation of settlements, as well as co-ordinated agricultural and farming activities. In addition to the anthropogenic influence on the environment identified since the Early Neolithic (SÜMEGI *et al.* 2003) such as soil erosion, plant cultivation and slash-and-burn deforestation, it has been presumed that parallel cultural processes in the Carpathian Basin also began as early as the 7th millennium BC (SÜMEGI 2004). Nevertheless, these human-induced environmental changes – as well as hunting – must have taken place on a microlevel during the Neolithic and the Copper Age, in comparison with the severe intervention characteristic of recent centuries, such as extensive deforestation, drainage and agricultural projects, which have affected avifaunas drastically. These interferences, together with the increasing exploitation of natural resources and the expansion of urban areas, resulted in the partial or complete extinction of several species and the adaptation of others to human habitats (GÁL 2003).

Since avian remains collected from Neolithic and Chalcolithic deposits reflect the precision of archaeological excavations as much as the preferences of prehistoric people, direct comparisons to recent avifaunas would be potentially misleading. Nevertheless, hunted birds once formed part of the ancient fauna and thus offer important information regarding the prehistoric distribution of the species in question.

All 19 species identified from the Neolithic period of Romania also occurred among the 56 species identified from the richer Chalcolithic deposits. As mentioned earlier, the remains of birds living in wetlands and steppes and diurnal birds of prey were the most frequent in the studied assemblages. Of the

56 species identified, only a few – whooper swan, teal, bean goose and the lesser white-fronted goose – do not breed in Romania (*Table 4*). The recent avifauna of Romania includes 300–400 species. 144 species of European conservation concern (SPECs) regularly breed in the country. Seven of these species are globally threatened (MUNTEANU 2000), among which the ferruginous duck, the spotted eagle, the imperial eagle and the great bustard have been identified from the archaeological sites under study. The ancient and recurrent presence of globally and nationally endangered species is summarised in *Table 12*.

Most fish-eating species, such as the cormorant, the grey heron and other large wading birds, so frequent in the ancient deposits, are considered today by fishermen to be as troublesome as vermin. A marked decline in the breeding range due to disturbance and persecution by humans and the drainage of nesting grounds have been noted in the case of the white pelican, whose breeding area is now confined to the Danube Delta, though it extended as far as the city of Călăraşi (lying in the vicinity of the Neolithic site of Grădiştea–Coslogeni) at the end of the 19th century. The Chalcolithic settlement of Vităneşti is the most distant inland site where remains of this species have been found (*Fig. 1*).

Bearded vulture, recorded from one Chalcolithic site (Vităneşti) only, used to breed in the Carpathians. The last specimen was shot in 1927, but the species was said to be present in Maramureş (Northern Romania) between 1935–1940. Ornithological work on the avifauna of Dobrogea, completed at the end of the 19th century, does not mention this species (ALMÁSY 1898). Marked contractions in range have been noted throughout Europe, and today the bearded vulture is extinct in many of the areas where it had nested during the 19th century (CRAMP 1998).

The white-tailed eagle, often identified from ancient habitations, was rather frequent along the Danube until the 20th century, breeding in "every" willow-wooded island (ALMÁSY 1898: 113). Today it is a rare but regular breeder in the Lower Danube Valley and the Danube Delta (MUNTEANU 1998: 17). The golden eagle, identified from one Neolithic (Isaccea–Suhat) and one Chalcolithic site (Hârşova), has been recently found nesting in the Carpathian Mountains only. There are probably no more than 30 breeding pairs (MUNTEANU 1998: 19). The spotted eagle also used to breed in Romania, but it has recently become a passage species (RADU 1983: 133).

The black grouse was identified from two Neolithic and three Chalcolithic sites in South-East Romania. Its numbers have continuously been decreasing in recent centuries (CRAMP 1998), and the breeding grounds have been confined

Table 12. Presence of globally and nationally endangered species in the Neolithic and Calcolithic assemblages, as well as in the recent avifauna of Romania and Hungary (* indicates the number of wintering individuals). Data on recent populations originate from BirdLife International 2004.

Scientific name	English Name	No. of archaeological sites in South-East Romania	No. of currently breeding pairs in Romania	No. of archaeological sites in the Great Hungarian Plain	No. of currently breeding pairs in Hungary
Botaurus stellaris	Bittern	1	1,500–2,000	2	700–1,000
Ardea purpurea	Purple heron	3	850–1,000	5	900–1,500
Ciconia nigra	Black stork	2 (?)	160–250	4	210–280
Ciconia ciconia	White stork	2	4,000–5,000	1 + 2 (?)	4,800–5,600
Anser erythropus	Lesser white-fronted goose	1 (?)	31–50*		0–20*
Anas acuta	Pintail	3	0–3	1	30–50
Aythya nyroca	Ferruginous duck	1	5,500–6,500	6	550–1,000
Haliaeetus albicilla	White-tailed eagle	5	28–33	7	60–100
Circaetus gallicus	Short-toed eagle		220–300	1	30–50
Circus macrourus	Pallid harrier	1	0–6		0
Aquila pomarina	Lesser spotted eagle	2	2,500–2,800	1	30–60
Aquila clanga	Spotted eagle	1	0–2		0
Aquila heliaca	Imperial eagle	1	5–10		50–65
Hieraaetus pennatus	Booted eagle	3	80–120	1	0–4
Perdix perdix	Partridge	3	120,000–180,000	2	14,000–33,000
Otis tarda	Great bustard	7	0–5	5	1,100–1,200
Bubo bubo	Eagle owl		750–1,000	1	10–30
Coracias garrulus	Roller		4,600–6,500	1	400–700
Alauda arvensis	Skylark		460,000–850,000	1	730,000–900,000

to the northern part of the Eastern Carpathians (RADU 1983). Current surveys give an account of 60–80 breeding pairs in Romania (BIRDLIFE INTERNATIONAL 2004).

The natural habitat of many steppe species has also decreased due to drainage (i.e. river regulations), in an effort to cultivate natural grassland. The crane, one of the most hunted species in the past, passed through in great numbers around the end of March during the 19th–20th centuries and used to breed in the deltas and lagoons of the region (ALMÁSY 1898: 116; RADU 1983: 109). Nowadays, two breeding pairs at most are known in Romania (BIRDLIFE INTERNATIONAL 2004). The demoiselle crane has always been considered a rare bird in this region; it was identified at Vităneşti only. Recently, this species has been recorded exclusively in Dobrudgea, and even there mostly during the spring (MUNTEANU 1998: 23).

The great bustard, rather frequent on the Romanian Lowland in the 7th millennium BC, was not identified from Dobrudgea, as it was not frequently seen there by Almásy at the end of the 19th century (ALMÁSY 1898: 117). Currently, rare migrants passing to their wintering areas in Bulgaria occur in this region. The great bustard, confined to the westernmost part of Romania, has decreased markedly since the 1960s and has become almost extinct (MUNTEANU 1998: 24).

The little bustard, found in the Chalcolithic deposits in the Romanian Lowland and the westernmost edge of Dobrudgea, used to breed in South-East Romania as well as in Moldova. Nowadays, this species occurs occasionally in passage (MUNTEANU 1998: 23). In addition, the breeding pairs of black stork, pintail and pallid harrier are also rather low in number (*Table 12*).

Inversely, from a chronological point of view, Early Neolithic assemblages yielded most of the 66 avian species identified from the territory of present-day Hungary. Naturally, this also reflects differences in sampling, since this period was better represented among the sites studied from this region. Only the eagle owl, identified from the Late Neolithic, and the whooper swan, the goshawk and the golden eagle, identified from the Copper Age, represent additional species to birds known from the intensively studied Körös culture period. Similarly to fowl identified from South-East Romania, most of the species are birds living in wetland and grassland environments. A smaller number of diurnal birds of prey and a larger number of songbirds have been recognized in Hungary. The only species that do not occur in the breeding season are the black-throated diver, the Slavonian grebe, the Barnacle goose and the goosander; the other species have either recently or formerly nested in the country (*Table 7–9*). Currently, there have been 125 species of European conservation concern breeding regularly in Hungary, of which five are globally threatened. In addition, there is a greater number of species which are in adverse conditions both in Hungary and Europe (NAGY 2000: 335; HARASZTHY 2003). Ferruginous duck and great bustard from the first category, as well as bittern, purple heron, black stork, white stork, pintail, white-tailed eagle, short-toed eagle, lesser spotted eagle, booted eagle, partridge, eagle owl, roller and skylark from the second group have been identified from both Neolithic and Copper Age deposits.

The breeding behaviour of a number of species has changed in Hungary as well. Whooper swans used to breed here until the 18th century; white pelicans, mute swans, black grouse and cranes until the 19th century. The little bustard became a rare migratory species only from the 20th century onwards (PETERSON *et al.* 1977; CRAMP 1998).

Interestingly, the remains of corncrake (*Crex crex*), a rather common breeding species both in Romania and Hungary today, were not identified from the archaeological assemblages under scrutiny. Living in wet meadows and cultivated areas, it has been a common species in both countries since the end of the 19th century (ALMÁSY 1898: 121; CHERNEL 2003). Currently, approximately 10,000–20,000 pairs have been reported from 52 areas of Romania (GACHE 1999: 1), while some 500–1200 pairs are breeding in Hungary (BIRDLIFE INTERNATIONAL 2004).

Nevertheless, according to a recent analysis considering the relationships between sample size and taxonomic richness in bone assemblages from prehistoric archaeological sites in Hungary, both the identified mammal and bird species made up only one-third of the number of known Holocene species. In the case of birds, the missing two-thirds from the archaeological record may also be related to the seasonal presence of a great number of species, rather than human selection (BARTOSIEWICZ – GÁL 2007).

10. Conclusions

Continuous and intensive excavations since the 1990s, especially in South-East Romania, provided an increasing number of avian bone assemblages from the areas under study. The application of modern excavation methods, such as water-sieving and dry screening, resulted in the recovery of previously ignored small animal remains, including tiny bird bones. Nevertheless, it is worth emphasising that the type and size of the sites, as well as the interest and care of archaeologists and archaeozoologists are always determining factors in the quantity of bird remains that are collected and discriminated.

The identification of avian remains found in recent years and the integration of the results with previously published data have offered the possibility of revising our knowledge on fowling during the Neolithic and Chalcolithic periods in two geographically similar regions. As evidenced by the recovered non-avian bones, meat provisioning was already based on animal husbandry at most of sites in these prehistoric periods, but hunting and other seasonal activities, such as gathering, fishing and fowling, also contributed to the food supply of the inhabitants. Fishing turned out to be rather important at a number of sites both in South-East Romania and the Great Hungarian Plain due to the proximity of rivers, although dissimilar methods of recovery may have resulted in biased sampling and thereby evaluation One must take into account, however, that even a considerable number of fish and bird remains represent only a small portion of the meat provided by animal husbandry, owing to the great number of bones making up a fish skeleton and the relatively small size of fish and bird compared with those of domestic mammals.

There is a remarkable difference between the Neolithic and Chalcolithic avian assemblages in both regions under study, but in a different way. While Neolithic deposits were strongly underrepresented by only five sites and 19 bird species in South-East Romania, 57 species from a total of 10 Chalcolithic tell settlements provided substantial information on bird hunting in the same region. The species composition from Chalcolithic sites covers data from the Neolithic completely, in the sense that all avian species identified from the Neolithic re-occurred in Chalcolithic assemblages as well.

The situation was the opposite in the Great Hungarian Plain. Neolithic – and especially 12 Early Neolithic (Körös culture) – sites offered most of the information on fowling, the Chalcolithic being represented by four sites only. None of the 12 bird taxa identified from the latter period provided new species, with respect to the 62 species described from Neolithic sites. These comparisons between assemblages of differing sizes suggest that sampling may have had as much influence on taxonomic composition as the geographical region or chronological affiliation.

The geographical location of the Great Hungarian Plain is similar to that of South-East Romania, the only difference being the proximity of the Black Sea and the Danube Delta in the latter case, which defines the migration routes of several species. The sites are located on broadly extended lowlands of loess ground, highly fragmented by a number of rivers and their branches, resulting in a mosaic-like environment. Geo-archaeological, archaeobotanical and archaeozoological investigations all offer evidence that prehistoric settlements often served as island-like refuges during the flood season.

In accordance with these ecological conditions, birds living in fresh water and adjacent environments, such as marshland and gallery forests, dominate both regions and periods under study. Exceptions are few and far between. Grebes, swans, ducks and coot were the most frequent among the aquatic species. Cormorants, large wading birds and diurnal birds of prey inhabited the gallery forests. Geese, partridges, cranes and bustards represent wild fowl living in wet and dry steppes. A number of diurnal birds of prey, black grouse and corvids were the most frequent species in the forest-steppe environment. Birds living in woodland, such as woodpigeons, thrushes and certain diurnal birds of prey, were the most under-represented in both Neolithic and Chalcolithic bone assemblages.

Nevertheless, differences in the frequency of certain bird groups could be perceived in the best-represented assemblages. A noteworthy abundance of ducks and woodland species were observed at the Körös culture settlement of Ecsegfalva 23 in the Great Hungarian Plain. The contemporaneous site of Endrőd 3/6 also yielded various duck species. Most of the steppe fowl were identified from Endrőd 119. Waterfowl dominated in the assemblages identified from the Gumelnița culture tell settlements of Borduşani Popină and Hârşova. In addition, forest-steppe species and birds peculiar to gallery forests were also frequent at these sites. The best-represented site in the region, Hârşova, is characterized by numerous diurnal birds of prey, as well as the notable absence of the crane and the great bustard. The Vităneşti tell is the only site in South-East Romania where steppe species were more frequent than birds living in wetland habitats. Remains from the black grouse and the great bustard were especially frequent in comparison with the other species.

Considering the seasonal characteristics of identified birds, the presence of unossified skeletal parts in bone assemblages and egg shell finds (not detailed in this volume), fowling was mostly practiced during the spring and summer. Winter visitor species – occurring exclusively in the cold season in South-East Romania such as Bewick's – or the tundra – swan, the whooper swan and the teal – suggest that the Gumelnița culture settlements of Borduşani Popină, Căscioarele, Hârşova and Vitănești were sites inhabited year-round. Similar conclusions may be drawn concerning the Körös culture sites of Ecsegfalva 23, Endrőd 119 and Nagykörü Tsz., from where the goosander, the Slavonian grebe and the barnacle goose were identified.

As supported by the evidence of remains from the aforementioned species, bird hunting must have been an opportunistic and typically seasonal activity. It is likely that fowling was often linked to similar activities, such as hunting, gathering and fishing. Considering the type of birds represented and the traces of butchery, burning and gnawing, it may be presumed that most of the birds were eaten. The majority of the burnt or even carbonized skeletal parts came from medium- and large-sized species, considered tasty even today; thus it is likely that these bones were burnt during the preparation of bird meat. Aside from the most frequently eaten types of fowl such as goose-like birds (Anseriformes), gallinaceous birds (Galliformes) and cranes and their relatives (Gruiformes), species from the orders of pelican-like birds (Pelecaniformes), heron and their relatives (Ciconiiformes), diurnal birds of prey (Accipitriformes) and song birds (Passeriformes) may also have been consumed.

The utilization of body parts such as the wings and feet/toes is also presumed on the basis of certain bone frequencies. The tip of the wings, especially from woodpigeons, seems to have been appreciated at the Körös culture settlement of Ecsegfalva 23. The distal part of the wing and legs from a number of diurnal birds of prey were possibly used for non-food purposes at the Gumelnița culture site of Hârşova. Bone representation in large and at least partially wet-screened deposits allowed the hypotheses considering the transport of entire (Borduşani Popină and Hârşova) or partially disarticulated (Ecsegfalva 23) birds to these settlements. One advantage of hand-collecting is that it may reveal fortunate conditions of accumulation. In fact, owing to the lack of screening, the carefully recorded spatial distribution of non-articulated bones, probably representing a few individuals at Vitănești, indicated that complete bodies of fowl were brought to the habitation.

In addition to meat, feathers could not only be used in housekeeping (e.g. as feather dusters or brushes), but were also given a role in decoration and ritual activities, as well as in fledging arrows, giving signals, etc. The skin and oil of birds may also have been a valuable raw material. Two long bird bone blanks from Hârşova and Vitănești also evidence the use of avian raw materials in craft activities.

Avian remains made up only a small proportion of the entire recovered animal bone assemblages and were massively under-represented in comparison with mammalian remains (they also fall behind fish remains at sites where wet-screening was applied). Nevertheless, when the taxonomic richness was compared to the diversity of wild mammals, bird bone assemblages seemed richer in taxonomic terms both in South-East Romania and the Great Hungarian Plain, which can be explained by the greater number of bird species as compared to (medium- and large sized) mammals in Holocene faunas.

The numbers of identified bird species from prehistoric deposits in South-East Romania (57) and East-Hungary (66) are rather close to each other. The recent avifauna consisting of 300–400 species in both countries also reflect comparable proportions. Major differences between the number of identified species from archaeological sites and their recent numbers are rather due to the seasonal presence of various species than to culturally idiosyncratic human selection.

Species that have been identified in deposits from Hungary and which have not yet been recognized in archaeological assemblages in Romania include the following: black-throated diver, little grebe, Slavonian grebe, spoonbill, white-fronted goose, Barnacle goose, wigeon, shoveler, scaup, goosander, short-toed eagle, marsh harrier, woodcock, black-tailed godwit, herring gull, eagle owl, roller, great spotted woodpecker, skylark, blackbird, mistle thrush, jay, starling and house sparrow, as well as the *Acrocephalus* genus, representing a warbler species. On the other hand, certain species have been identified in Romania, but are missing from the archaeozoological lists in Hungary. These species are the following: black-necked grebe, glossy ibis, honey buzzard, bearded vulture, pallid harrier, spotted eagle, imperial eagle, osprey, peregrine, demoiselle crane, short-eared owl, hoopoe, sand martin, barn swallow, fieldfare and raven.

By the identification of bird bones from archaeological deposits, important information can be also gained regarding the ancient presence of certain species, which are endangered or extinct today. The ferruginous duck and the great bustard, which have become globally threatened, were identified from a number of sites both in South-East Romania and the Great Hungarian Plain. Moreover, the globally threatened spotted eagle and imperial eagle have been identified from South-East Romania. The bearded vulture and the little bustard are extinct now in Romania, while the golden eagle can be found in small numbers in the Carpathian Mountains only. The numbers of breeding pairs of the pintail, the pallid harrier, the spotted eagle, the crane, the Demoiselle crane and the great bustard have also decreased to a minimum. In Hungary, the black grouse and the little bustard have become extinct, while the crane, which used to breed here as late as the end of the 19th century, now appears as a spring and autumn passage species.

References

ALMÁSY, GY. V. 1898
   Madártani betekintés a román Dobrudsába. Ornithologische Recognoscirung der Rumänischen Dobrudscha. *Aquila* 5, 1–207.

ANDREESCU, R. R., MIREA, P. – APOPE, ŞT. 2003
   Cultura Gumelniţa în vestul Munteniei. Aşezarea de la Vităneşti, jud. Teleorman (La culture Gumelniţa a l'ouest de Muntenia). *Cercetări Arheologice* 12, 71–87.

BAGYURA, J., SCHMIDT, A., LÁZÁR, V., SZITTA, T., FIRMÁNSZKY, G. – SÁNDOR, I. 2006
   A különleges Madárvédelmi Területeken (SPA) fészkelő fokozottan védett nappali ragadozó madarak és az uhu állomány felmérése [Survey of the extensively protected diurnal birds of prey and eagle owl nesting in Specially Protected Areas (SPAs)]. *Heliaca* 2004, 23–27.

BĂLĂŞESCU, A. 2003a
   Cercetări de anatomie comparată asupra faunei din aşezările neolitice din sud-estul României [Comparative anatomical studies on the faunas from Neolithic settlements from South-East Romania]. PhD Thesis. Iaşi, Universitatea "Al. I. Cuza".

BĂLĂŞESCU, A. 2003b
   L'étude de la faune des mammifères découverts a Luncaviţa. *Peuce* 14, 449–468.

BĂLĂŞESCU, A. – RADU, V. 2002
   Culesul, pescuitul şi vânătoarea în cultura Boian pe teritoriul României (La cueilette, la pêche et la chasse dans la culture Boian sur le territoire de la Roumanie). *Studii de Preistorie* 1, 73–94.

BĂLĂŞESCU, A. – RADU, V. 2003
   Studiul materialului faunistic descoperit în *Tell*-ul Vităneşti (jud. Teleorman): nivelul Gumelniţa B_1 (L'étude du matériel de faune découvert sur le tell de Vităneşti). *Cercetări Arheologice* 12, 363–385.

BĂLĂŞESCU, A., MOISE, D. – DUMITRAŞCU, V. 2003
Mammal fauna from Borduşani–Popină. In: Popovici, D. (ed.), *Archaeological pluridisciplinary researches at Borduşani-Popină.* 103–140, 190–191. Editura Cetatea de Scaun, Bucureşti.

BĂLĂŞESCU, A., MOISE, D. – RADU, V. 2005
The palaeoeconomy of Gumelniţa communities on the territoty of Romania. *Cultură şi Civilizaţie la Dunărea de Jos* 22, 167–206.

BANNER, J. 1940
Hódmezővásárhely története a honfoglalás koráig. Első rész: A legrégibb időktől a bronzkor kialakulásáig [The history of Hódmezővásárhely until the Period of the Hungarian Conquest. Part 1: From the earliest times until the beginning of the Bronze Age]. Hódmezővásárhely, Hódmezővásárhelyi Múzeum.

BÁNFFY, E. 1997
Cult objects of the Neolithic Lengyel culture. Budapest, Archaeolingua.

BARTOSIEWICZ, L. 2001
Archaeozoology or zooarchaeology? A problem from the last century. *Archaeologica Polona* 39, 71–86.

BARTOSIEWICZ, L. 2005
Plain talk: animals, environment and culture in the Neolithic of the Carpathian Basin and adjacent areas. In: Bailey, D. – Whittle, A. (eds.), *(Un)settling the Neolithic.* 51–63. Oxbow Books, Oxford.

BARTOSIEWICZ, L. 2007a (in print)
Mammalian bone. In: Whittle, A. (ed.), *The Early Neolithic on the Great Hungarian Plain: investigations of the Körös culture site of Ecsegfalva 23, County Békés.* Archaeological Institute of the Hungarian Academy of Sciences, Budapest.

BARTOSIEWICZ, L. 2007b (in print)
Fish remains. In: Whittle, A. (ed.), *The Early Neolithic on the Great Hungarian Plain: investigations of the Körös culture site of Ecsegfalva 23, County Békés.* Archaeological Institute of the Hungarian Academy of Sciences, Budapest.

BARTOSIEWICZ, L. 2007c (in print)
Alföld Linearband culture animal remains from the settlement of Debrecen–Nyulas, Eastern Hungary. *Ősrégészeti Levelek – Prehistoric Newsletters* 9.

BARTOSIEWICZ, L. – GÁL, E. 2007
A mintanagyság és a fajgazdagság összefüggése régészeti emlős- és madármintákban (Relationships between sample size and taxonomic richness in mammalian and bird bone assemblages from archaeological sites). Meeting of the Archaeometry Workshop "Miklós Kretzoi and the interdisciplinary relations of the archaeology". Budapest (Hungary), 12th February 2007. http://www.ace.hu/ametry/am070212/AM2007-1-blh.html

BEM, C. 2000
Elemente de cronologie radiocarbon. Ariile culturale Boian–Gumelnița–Cernavoda I și Precucuteni–Cucuteni/Tripolie (Éléments de chronologie radiocarbone. Les zones culturelles Boian-Gumelnița-Cernavodă I et Precucuteni-Cucuteni/Tripolie). *Cercetări Arheologice* 11, 337–359.

BEM, C. 2001
Noi propuneri pentru o schiță cronologică a Eneoliticului românesc (Chronological scheme of the Romanian Chalcolithic). *Pontica* 33-34, 25–121.

BENDA, B. 2004
Étkezési szokások a 17. századi főúri udvarokban Magyarországon. PhD Thesis. Budapest, Eötvös Loránd Universitiy.

BENDA, B. – VÁRKONYI, G. 2001
„*Az asszony dolga guzsaly s motolla…*". *Rákóczi Erzsébet levelei férjéhez, 1672–1707* ["A lady's business are distaff and reel": Erzsébet Rákóczi's letters to her husband, 1672–1707]. Budapest, Osiris.

BIRDLIFE INTERNATIONAL 2004
Birds in Europe: population estimates, trends and conservation status. Cambridge, BirdLife International.

B. KUTZIÁN, I. 1958
Polgár–Csőszhalom. *Régészeti Füzetek* 10, 16.

BOVY, K. M. 2002
Differential avian skeletal part distribution: explaining the abundance of wings. *Journal of Archaeological Science* 29, 965–978.

BÖKÖNYI, S. 1959
Die frühalluviale Wirbeltierfauna Ungarns. *Acta Archaeologica Academiae Scientiarum Hungaricae* 11, 39–102.

BÖKÖNYI, S. 1964
A maroslele-panai neolitikus telep gerinces faunája (The vertebrate fauna of the Neolithic settlement at Maroslele–Pana). *Archeológiai Értesítő* 91, 87–93.

BÖKÖNYI, S. 1974
History of domestic mammals in Central and Eastern Europe. Budapest, Akadémiai Kiadó.

BÖKÖNYI, S. 1989
Animal husbandry of the Körös-Starčevo complex: its origin and development. In: Bökönyi, S. (ed.), *Neolithic of Southeastern Europe and its Near Eastern connections.* 13–16. Archaeological Institute of the Hungarian Academy of Sciences, Budapest.

BÖKÖNYI, S. 1992a
Early Neolithic vertebrate fauna of Endrőd 119. In: Bökönyi, S. (ed.), *Cultural and Landscape Changes in South-East Hungary, I. Reports on the Gyomaendrőd Project.* 195–299. Archaeolingua, Budapest.

BÖKÖNYI, S. 1992b
Foreword. In: Bökönyi, S. (ed.), *Cultural and Landscape Changes in South-East Hungary, I. Reports on the Gyomaendrőd Project.* 7–8. Archaeolingua, Budapest.

BÖKÖNYI, S. – JÁNOSSY, D. 1965
Szubfosszilis vadmadár-leletek Magyarországon (Subfossile Wildvogelfunde aus Ungarn). *Vertebrata Hungarica* 7, 85–99.

CASSOLI, P. F. – TAGLIACOZZO, A. 1997
Butchering and cooking of birds in the Palaeolithic site of Grotta Romanelli (Italy). *International Journal of Osteoarchaeology* 7, 303–320.

CHERNEL, I. 2003
Magyarország madarai [Birds of Hungary]. CD-RM. Budapest, Arcanum.

CHOYKE, A. M. 2001
OLate Neolithic Red Deer Canine Beads and Their Imitations. In: Choyke, A. M. – Bartosiewicz, L. (eds.), *Crafting Bone – Skeletal Technologies through Time and Space.* 251–266. Archaeopress, Oxford.

CIMEC 1994

Raport de cercetare arheologică: Ciulnița. In: cIMeC – Institutul de Memorie Culturală (ed.), *Cronica Cercetărilor Arheologice*. Institutul de Memorie Culturală, București. http://www.cimec.ro/scripts/arh/cronica/detaliu.asp?k=76

CIMEC 1995

Raport de cercetare arheologică: Insurăței. In: cIMeC – Institutul de Memorie Culturală (ed.), *Cronica Cercetărilor Arheologice*. Institutul de Memorie Culturală, București. http://www.cimec.ro/scripts/arh/cronica/detaliu.asp?k=1634

CIMEC 1996

Raport de cercetare arheologică: Vitănești tell. In: cIMeC – Institutul de Memorie Culturală (ed.), *Cronica Cercetărilor Arheologice*. Institutul de Memorie Culturală, București. http://www.cimec.ro/scripts/arh/cronica/detaliu.asp?k=464

CIMEC 1997a

Raport de cercetare arheologică: Grădiștea–Coslogeni. In: cIMeC – Institutul de Memorie Culturală (ed.), *Cronica Cercetărilor Arheologice*. Institutul de Memorie Culturală, București. http://www.cimec.ro/scripts/arh/cronica/detaliu.asp?k=505

CIMEC 1997b

Raport de cercetare arheologică: Vitănești tell. In: cIMeC – Institutul de Memorie Culturală (ed.), *Cronica Cercetărilor Arheologice*. Institutul de Memorie Culturală, București. http://www.cimec.ro/scripts/arh/cronica/detaliu.asp?k=577

CIMEC 1998

Raport de cercetare arheologică: Hârșova tell. In: cIMeC – Institutul de Memorie Culturală (ed.), *Cronica Cercetărilor Arheologice*. Institutul de Memorie Culturală, București. http://www.cimec.ro/scripts/arh/cronica/detaliu.asp?k=1620

CIMEC 1999

Raport de cercetare arheologică: Năvodari. In: cIMeC – Institutul de Memorie Culturală (ed.), *Cronica Cercetărilor Arheologice*. Institutul de Memorie Culturală, București. http://www.cimec.ro/scripts/arh/cronica/detaliu.asp?k=919

CIMEC 2000a
Raport de cercetare arheologică: Grădiştea–Coslogeni. In: cIMeC – Institutul de Memorie Culturală (ed.), *Cronica Cercetărilor Arheologice.* Institutul de Memorie Culturală, Bucureşti. http://www.cimec.ro/scripts/arh/cronica/detaliu.asp?k=1038

CIMEC 2000b
Raport de cercetare arheologică: Panduru. In: cIMeC – Institutul de Memorie Culturală (ed.), *Cronica Cercetărilor Arheologice.* Institutul de Memorie Culturală, Bucureşti. http://www.cimec.ro/scripts/arh/cronica/detaliu.asp?k=1286

CIMEC 2001
Raport de cercetare arheologică: Gălăţui–Movila Berzei. In: cIMeC – Institutul de Memorie Culturală (ed.), *Cronica Cercetărilor Arheologice.* Institutul de Memorie Culturală, Bucureşti. http://www.cimec.ro/scripts/arh/cronica/detaliu.asp?k=1372

CIMEC 2004a
Raport de cercetare arheologică: Măgura–Buduiasca. In: cIMeC – Institutul de Memorie Culturală (ed.), *Cronica Cercetărilor Arheologice.* Institutul de Memorie Culturală, Bucureşti. http://www.cimec.ro/scripts/arh/cronica/detaliu.asp?k=3171

CIMEC 2004b
Raport de cercetare arheologică: Bordușani–Popină. In: cIMeC – Institutul de Memorie Culturală (ed.), *Cronica Cercetărilor Arheologice.* Institutul de Memorie Culturală, Bucureşti. http://www.cimec.ro/scripts/arh/cronica/detaliu.asp?k=3074

CRAMP, S. 1998 (ed.)
The complete birds of the Western Palearctic on CD-ROM. Oxford, Oxford University Press.

CSENGERI, P. – PATAY, R. 2002
Mezőzombor, Községi temető [Mezőzombor, community cemetery]. In: Kisfaludi, J. (ed.), *Régészeti Kutatások Magyarországon 2001 (Archaeological Investigations in Hungary 2001).* 191. Kulturális Örökségvédelmi Hivatal és Magyar Nemzeti Múzeum, Budapest.

DANI, J. 2007 (in print)
Preliminary Report on the excavations at Debrecen–Nyulas ("Toyota-Szalon"), Eastern Hungary. *Ősrégészeti Levelek – Prehistoric Newsletters* 9.

DESSE-BERSET, N. – RADU, V. 1996
Stratégies d'échantillonnage et d'exploitation des restes osseux de poissons pour une approche paléoenvironnementale et paléoéconomique: l'exemple d'Hârşova Roumanie, (Néolithique final-Chalcolithique). In: Langouet, L. (ed.), *Actes du Colloque d'Archéométrie 1995, Périgueux (Dordogne, France)*. 181–186. Revue d'Archéométrie, Rennes.

DOMBORÓCZKY, L. 2004
Tiszaszőlős, Domaháza, Puszta-Réti-dűlő. In: Kisfaludi, J. (ed.), *Régészeti Kutatások Magyarországon 2003 (Archaeological Investigations in Hungary, 2003)*. 303–305. Budapest, Kulturális Örökségvédelmi Hivatal és Magyar Nemzeti Múzeum.

DRIESCH, A. von den 1976
A guide to the measurement of animal bones from archaeological sites. Cambridge, MA, Harvard University.

GACHE, C. 1999
Országos haris számlálás [National census of corncrakes in Hungary]. *Migrans* 3, 1.

GÁL, E. 2003
Adaptation of different bird species to human environments. In: Laszlovszky, J. – Szabó, P. (eds.), *People and Nature in a Historical*. 120–138. Central European University, Department of Medieval Studies – Archaeolingua, Budapest.

GÁL, E. 2004
The Neolithic avifauna of Hungary within the context of the Carpathian Basin. *Antaeus* 27, 273–286.

GÁL, E. 2005
New data to the bird bone artefacts from Hungary and Romania. In: Luik, H., Choyke, A. M., Batey, C. E. – Lõugas, L. (eds.), *From Hooves to Horns, from Mollusc to Mammoth. Manufacture and Use of Bone Artefacts from Prehistoric Times to the Present*. 325–338. Institute of History – University of Tartu, Tallinn.

GÁL, E. 2006a
The role of archaeo-ornithology in environmental and animal history studies. In: Jerem, E., Mester, Zs. – Benczes, R. (eds.), *Archaeological and Cultural Heritage Preservation Within the Light of New Technologies. Selected papers from the joint Archaeolingua–EPOCH workshop, 27th September–2nd October 2004, Százhalombatta, Hungary*. 49–61. Archaeolingua, Budapest.

GÁL, E. 2006b (in print)
Bird bone double pipe from the Avar cemetery of Szegvár–Szőlőkalja. In: Bende, L. – Lőrinczy, G. (eds.), *Das awarenzeitliche Gräberfeld in Szegvár–Szőlőkalja*. 145–147. Móra Ferenc Múzeum, Szeged.

GÁL, E. 2007a (in print)
Bird remains from archaeological sites around Lake Balaton. In: Zatykó, Cs., Juhász, I. – Sümegi, P. (eds.), *Environmental archaeology in Transdanubia*. 79–96. Archaeological Institute of the Hungarian Academy of Sciences, Budapest.

GÁL, E. 2007b (in print)
Bird remains. In: Whittle, A. (ed), *The Early Neolithic on the Great Hungarian Plain: investigations of the Körös culture site of Ecsegfalva 23, County Békés*. Archaeological Institute of the Hungarian Academy of Sciences, Budapest.

GÁL, E. 2007c (in print)
Bird bone remains from Bronze Age settlements in the Carpathian Basin. In: Poroszlai, I. – Vicze, M. (eds.), *Opinions on the Koszider Period*. MATRICA Múzeum, Százhalombatta.

GÁL, E. (forthcoming a)
"Fine feathers make fine birds": the exploitation of wild birds in medieval Hungary. In: Mulville, J. – Powell, A. (eds.), *"A walk on the wild side"*. Oxbow Books, Oxford.

GÁL, E. (forthcoming b)
Broken-winged: fossil and subfossil pathological bird bones from recent excavations. In: Homas, R. – Miklikova, Z. (eds.), *Proceedings of the 1st Meeting of the ICAZ Animal Palaeopathology Working Group, Nitra 23rd–24th September, 2004*. Archaeopress, Oxford.

GÁL, E. – KESSLER, E. 2002
Bird Remains from the Eneolithic and Iron Age Site Borduşani Popina and Eneolithic Site Hârşova (Southeast Romania). In: Bocheński, Z. M.,

Bocheński, Z. – Stewart, J. R. (eds.), *Proceedings of the 4th Meeting of the ICAZ Bird Working Group, Kraków, Poland, 11th–15th September, 2001.* 253–262. Institute of Animal Systematics and Evolution, Kraków.

GÁL, E. – KESSLER, E. 2003
Eneolithic bird remains from the tell site of Borduşani-Popină. In: Popovici, D. (ed.), *Archaeological pluridisciplinary researches at Borduşani-Popină.* 141–154, 192–193. Editura Cetatea de Scaun, Bucureşti.

GOTFREDSEN, A. B. – MØBJERG, T. 2004
Nipisat – a Saqqaq culture site in Sisimiut, Central West Greenland. Copenhagen, Danish Polar Center.

GUNDA, B. 1979
The gathering of the eggs of waterfowl in Hungary. In: Gunda, B. (ed.), *Ethnographica Carpatho-Balcanica.* 15–27. Akadémiai Kiadó, Budapest.

HARASZTHY, L. 2003 (ed.)
Veszélyeztetett madarak fajvédelmi tervei [Species protection plans for endangered birds]. Budapest, Magyar Madártani és Természetvédelmi Egyesület.

HORVÁTH, Z., BANK, L., KALOCSA, B., TÖMÖSVÁRY, T. – PINTÉR, A. 2006
Rétisas-védelmi Munkacsoport beszámolója [Report of the White-tailed Eagle Study Group]. *Heliaca* 2004, 20–22.

HAŞOTTI, P. – POPOVICI, D. 1992
Cultura Cernavodă I în contextul descoperirilor de la Hârşova (Die Cernavoda-Kultur im Kontext der Funde von Hârşova). *Pontica* 25, 15–44.

JÁNOSSY, D. 1985
Wildvogelreste aus archäologischen Grabungen in Ungarn (Neolithicum bis Mittelalter). *Fragmenta Mineralogica et Palaeontologica* 12, 67–103.

JURCSÁK, T. – KESSLER, E. 1986
Evoluţia avifaunei pe teritoriul României. I (The evolution of the avian fauna in the territory of Romania. Part 1). *Crisia* 16, 577–615.

JURCSÁK, T. – KESSLER, E. 1988
Evoluţia avifaunei pe teritoriul României. III (The evolution of the avian fauna in the territory of Romania. Part 3). *Crisia* 18, 647–688.

KALICZ, N. 1964
Tiszavasvári–Keresztfal. *Régészeti Füzetek* 17, 19.

KARDOS, L. 1943
Az Őrség népi táplálkozása [Traditional food in the Őrség region]. Budapest, Államtudományi Intézet Táj- és Népkutató Osztálya.

KEMENCZEI, T. 1968
Szerencs. *Régészeti Füzetek* 21, 16.

KESSLER, E. 1985
Contribuţii noi la studiul avifaunelor cuaternare din România (Nouvelles contributions á l'étude des avifaunes quaternaires de la Roumanie). *Crisia* 15, 485–491.

KESSLER, E. – GÁL, E. 1997
Aves. In: Marinescu-Bîlcu et al. (eds.), *Archaeological researches at Borduşani–Popină (Ialomiţa county). Preliminary report 1993–1994*. 108–109. Muzeul Naţional de Istorie a României, Bucureşti.

KODOLÁNYI, J. JR. 1976
North Eurasian hunting, fishing and reindeer-breeding civilizations. In: Hajdú, P. (ed.), *Ancient cultures of the uralian peoples*. 145–171. Corvina Press, Budapest.

KOREK, J. 1958
Lebő-halmi ásatás 1950-ben (The excavation at Lebőhalom in 1950). *Archeológiai Értesítő* 85, 132–155.

KOREK, J. 1971
Szegvár–Tűzköves. *Régészeti Füzetek* 24, 15.

KOREK, J. 1977
Az alföldi vonaldíszes kerámia népének települése Kisköre–Gáton (Die Siedlung des Volkes der Linearkeramik im Alföld auf dem Kisköre–Damm). *Archaeológiai Értesítő* 104, 3–17.

KOZÁK, J. 1997
Kettétört csontsípszár a Bijelo brdoi avarkori temetőben (Broken bone pipe from the Avar Period cemetery of Bielo Brdo). *Communicationes Archaeologicae Hungariae* 1997, 195–203.

LAKÓ, E. 1983
Bornemissza Anna szakácskönyve 1680-ból [Anna Bornemissza's cookery book from 1680]. Bukarest, Kriterion Könyvkiadó.

LIGETI, L. (transl. 1962).
A mongolok titkos története [The secret history of the Mongols]. Budapest, Gondolat Kiadó.

LYMAN, R. L. 1994
Vertebrate taphonomy. Cambridge, University Press.

MAKKAY, J. 1992
Excavations at the Körös culture settlement of Endrőd–Öregszőlők 199 in 1986–1989. In: Bökönyi, S. (ed.), *Cultural and Landscape Changes in South-East Hungary, I. Reports on the Gyomaendrőd Project.* 121–193. Archaeolingua, Budapest.

MAKKAY, J. 2007
Endrőd, site 3/6. In: Starnini, E. – Biagi, P. (eds.), *The excavation of the Early Neolithic sites of the Körös culture in the Körös Valley, Hungary: the final report. Vol. I, The excavations: stratigraphy, structures and graves.* 72–93. Società per la Preistoria e Protostoria della Regione Friuli-Venezia Giulia.

MANNERMAA, K. 2003
Birds in Finnish prehistory. *Fennoscandia archaeologica* 20, 3–40.

MANTU, C.-M. 1995
Câteva considerații privind cronologia absolută a neo-eneoliticului din România (Some considerations concerning the absolute chronology of the Neo-Aeneolithic in Romania). *Studii și Cercetări de Istorie Veche* 46, 213–235.

MARINESCU-BÎLCU, S. 1997
Historical background. In: Marinescu-Bîlcu et al. (eds.), *Archaeological researches at Borduşani-Popină (Ialomiţa county) Preliminary report 1993–1994.* 35–38. Muzeul Național de Istorie a României, București.

MICU, C., MICU, S., BĂLĂŞESCU, A., RADU, V., LUCA, G. – HAITĂ, G. 2000
Aşezarea neolitică de la Isaccea, punctul Suhat, jud. Tulcea (The Neolithic settlement from Isaccea–Suhat, Tulcea county). In: Iacob, M., Oberländer-Târnoveanu, E. – Topoleanu, F. (eds.), *Istro-Pontica.* 5–52. Consiliul Județean Tulcean, Tulcea.

MOISE, D. 1997

Mammals. In: Marinescu-Bîlcu et al. (eds.), *Archaeological researches at Borduşani–Popină (Ialomiţa county). Preliminary report 1993–1994*. 110–127. Muzeul Naţional de Istorie a României, Bucureşti.

MOISE, D. 1999

Studiul materialului faunistic aparţinând mamiferelor, descoperit în locuinţele gumelniţene de la Însurăţei-Popina I (jud. Brăila) (Étude du matériel faunique [mammifères] découvert dans les habitations type Gumelnitza, à Însurăţei-Tell I, [dép. de Brăila]). *Istros* 9, 171–190.

MOISE, D. 2000

Étude du matériel ostéologique appartenant aux mammifères découvert dans le Complexe 521 (dépotoire) sur le tell néo-énéolitique de Hârşova (dép. de Constantza). *Cercetări arheologice* 11, 84–111.

MOISE, D. 2001a

Aşezarea eneolitică de pe insula „La Ostrov", Lacul Taşaul (Năvodari, jud. Constanţa). Raport preliminar – Campaniile 1999–2000. Studiul materialului osteologic de mamifere (L'étude du matériel ostéologique de mammifères provenant du tell énéolithique de l'île 'La Ostrov' (Năvodari, lac Taşaul, dép. de Constanţa). Campagnes 1999 – 2000. *Pontica* 33–34, 156–164.

MOISE, D. 2001b

Studiul materialului faunistic provenit din aşezarea eneolitică de la Măriuţa (jud. Călăraşi) (L'étude du matériel faunistique de l'habitat énéolithique de Măriuţa sur l'habitat). *Cultură şi Civilizaţie la Dunărea de Jos* 16–17, 207–222.

MUNTEANU, D. 1998

The status of birds in Romania. Cluj Napoca, Romanian Ornithological Society.

MUNTEANU, D. 2000

Romania. In: Heath, M. F. – Evans, M. I. (eds.), *Important bird areas in Europe: priority sites for conservation. Volume 2: Southern Europe*. 481–501. BirdLife International, Cambridge.

NAGY, SZ. 2000

Hungary. In: Heath, M. F. – Evans, M. I. (eds.), *Important bird areas in Europe: priority sites for conservation. Volume 2: Southern Europe*. 335–355. BirdLife International, Cambridge.

O'CONNOR, T. P. 2000
The archaeology of animal bones. Phoenix Mill, Sutton Publishing Ltd.

ORTUTAY, GY. 1977
Magyar néprajzi lexikon [Encyclopaedia of Hungarian Ethnography]. Budapest, Akadémiai Kiadó.

PATAY, P. 1966
Kisköre–Szingegát. *Régészeti Füzetek* 20, 16.

PATAY, P. 1969
Tiszavalk–Négyesi határ. *Régészeti Füzetek* 22, 23.

PATAY, P. 1975
Tiszavalk–Tetes. *Régészeti Füzetek* 28, 24.

PATAY, P. 1971
Die jüngere Stein- und die Kupferzeit im Südlichen Teil des Komitates Borsod. *Acta Antiqua et Archaeologica* 14, 7–15.

PATAY, P. 1978
A Tiszavalk–Tetesi rézkori temető és telep (Kupferzeitliches Gräberfeld und Siedlung von Tiszavalk–Tetes. *Folia Archaeologica* 29, 21–55.

PATAY, P. 1987
A tiszalúc–sarkadi rézkori telep ásatásának eddigi eredményei (Bisherige Ergebnisse der Ausgrabung in der kupferzeitlichen Siedlung von Tiszalúc–Sarkad). *Folia Archaeologica* 38, 89–120.

PÁK, D. 1829
Vadászattudomány [The science of hunting]. Buda, Magyar Királyi Tudományi Egyetem.

PETERSON, R. T., MOUNTFORT, G. – HOLLOM, P. A. D. 1977
Európa madarai [The birds of Europe]. Budapest, Gondolat Kiadó.

PIKE-TAY, A. 2007 (in print)
Skeletochronological evidence for seasonal culling of caprines. In: Whittle, A. (ed.) *The Early Neolithic on the Great Hungarian Plain: investigations of the Körös culture site of Ecsegfalva 23, County Békés*. Archaeological Institute of the Hungarian Academy of Sciences, Budapest.

PIKE-TAY, A., BARTOSIEWICZ, L., GÁL, E. – WHITTLE, A. 2004
Body-part representation and seasonality: sheep/goat, bird and fish remains from early Neolithic Ecsegfalva 23, SE Hungary. *Journal of Taphonomy* 2, 221–246.

POPOVICI, D., RANDOIN, B., RIALLAND, Y., VOINEA, V., VLAD, F., BEM, C., BEM, C. – HAITĂ, G. 2000.
Objectifs. In: Popovici, D. (ed.), *Les recherches archéologiques du tell de Hârşova (dép. De Constanţa) 1997-1998.* 13–34. Muzeul Naţional de Istorie a României, Bucureşti.

RACZKY, P. 1975
Kőtelek. *Régészeti Füzetek* 28, 13.

RACZKY, P., SÜMEGI, P., BARTOSIEWICZ, L., GÁL, E., KACZANOWSKA, M., KOZŁOWSKI, J. K. – ANDERS, A. 2007 (in print)
Ecological barrier versus mental marginal zone? Problems of the northernmost Körös culture settlements in the Great Hungarian Plain. In: Gronenborg, D. (ed.), *Die Neolithisierung Mitteleuropas – The Spread of the Neolithic to Central Europe.* Mainz.

RADU, D. 1983
Mic atlas ornitologic [Small ornithological atlas]. Bucureşti, Editura Albatros.

RADU, V. 1997
Pisces. In: Marinescu-Bîlcu et al. (eds.), *Archaeological researches at Borduşani–Popină (Ialomiţa county). Preliminary report 1993–1994.* 96–105. Muzeul Naţional de Istorie a României, Bucureşti.

RADU, V. 1999
Studiul resturilor osoase de peşte de la Insurăţei–Popina I A. Campaniile 1995–1998 (Étude des débris osseaux de poissons découverts à Însurăţei-Tell I A). *Istros* 9, 191–196.

RADU, V. 2000a
Studiul materialului arheoihtiologic de la Ciulniţa (jud. Ialomiţa) din nivelele Boian-Giuleşti. Campaniile 1994-1995 (L'étude du matériel archéo-ichtyologique Boian-Giuleşti de Ciulniţa [dép. de Ialomiţa]. Les campagnes de fouilles 1994-1995). *Ialomiţa – Studii şi comunicări de istorie, arheologie, etnografie* 3, 9–11.

RADU, V. 2000b
Sur la durée d'utilisation d'un dépotoir appartenant à la culture Gumelnița A2 du tell d'Hârșova. Étude archéologique préliminaire. In: Popovici, D. (ed.), *Les recherches archéologiques du tell de Hârșova (dép. de Constanța) 1997-1998.* 75–83. Muzeul Național de Istorie a României, București.

RADU, V. 2000c
Așezarea neolitică de la Isaccea, punctul Suhat, jud. Tulcea. Studiul preliminar al materialului arheoihtiologic din nivelele Boian-Giulești de la Isaccea (jud. Tulcea) (The Neolithic settlement from Isaccea–Suhat [Tulcea County]). In: Iacob, M., Oberländer-Târnoveanu, E. – Topoleanu, F. (eds.), *Istro-Pontica.* 13–16. Consiliul Județean Tulcea, Tulcea.

RADU, V. 2001a
Grădiștea Coslogeni. Studiul arheoihtiologic al materialului din nivelul neolitic (Grădiștea Coslogeni. Étude archéologique du matériel du niveau néolithique). *Cultura si Civilizație la Dunarea de Jos* 16–17, 184–189.

RADU, V. 2001b
Așezarea eneolitică de pe insula „La Ostrov", Lacul Tașaul (Năvodari, jud. Constanța). Raport preliminar – Campaniile 1999–2000. Studiul materialului arheoihtiologic (L'étude du matériel archéoichthyologique des niveaux Gumelnita de l'établissement Tașaul-tell [l'île "La Ostrov", Năvodari, dép. de Constanța]. Campagnes 1999 – 2000 résumé). *Pontica* 33-34, 165–170.

RADU, V. 2003a
Exploitation des ressources aquatiques dans les cultures néolithiques et calcolithiques de la Roumanie Méridionale. These de doctorat. Aix-en-Provence, Université Aix-Marseille I.

RADU, V. 2003b
Several data about fish and fishing importance in the palaeoeconomy of the Gumelnița A2 community from Borduşani–Popină. In: Popovici, D. (ed.), *Archaeological pluridisciplinary researches at Borduşani–Popină.* 159–171, 191–192. Editura Cetatea de Scaun, București.

RADU, V. 2003c
L'étude préliminaire du matériel archéo-ichtyologique provenant des niveaux Gumelnița A2 de l'établissement Luncavița–Cetățuie. *Peuce* 14, 449–468.

SCHUSTER, C. 2002

Einige Erwägungen bezüglich des Fischfangs in der Vorgeschichte an der Unteren Donau. *Cultura si civilizaţie la Dunarea de Jos* 19, 159–169.

SCHWARTZ, C. A. 1998

Animal bones from Polgár–Csőszhalom, Eastern Hungary. In: Anreiter, P., Bartosiewicz, L., Jerem, E. – Meid, W. (eds.) *Man and the Animal World. Studies in memoriam Sándor Bökönyi.* 511–514. Archaeolingua, Budapest.

SIDELL, E. J. 1993

A methodology for the identification of avian eggshell from archaeological sites. *Archaeofauna* 2, 45–51.

STALLIBRASS, S. 1990

The distinction between the effects of small carnivores and humans on postglacial faunal assemblages. In: Grigson, C. – Cutton-Brock, J. (eds.), *Animals and archaeology: 4. Husbandry in Europe.* 259–269. Archaeopress, Oxford.

SÜMEGI, P. 2004

Preneolitizáció – egy kárpát-medencei, késő mezolitikum során bekövetkezett életmódbeli változás környezettörténeti rekonstrukciója (Pre-neolitization – The environmental-historical reconstruction of a change in lifestyle occuring during the Late Mesoliticum in the Carpatjian Basin). *MÓMOSZ* 2, 21–32.

SÜMEGI, P., KERTÉSZ, R. – HERTELENDI, E. 2002

Environmental change and human adaptation in the Carpathian Basin at the Late Glacial/Postglacial transition. In: Jerem, E. – T. Biró, K. (eds.), *Archaeometry 98. Proceedings of the 31st Symposium, Budapest, 26th April–3rd May, 1998.* 171–177. Archaeolingua, Budapest.

SÜMEGI, P., KERTÉSZ, R. – RUDNER, E. 2003

Palaeoenvironmental history of Hungary. In: Visy, Zs. (ed.), *Hungarian Archaeology at the turn of the Millenium.* 51–56. Ministry of the Cultural Heritage, Teleki László Foundation, Budapest.

TAKÁCS, I. 1992

Fish remains from the early Neolithic site of Endrőd 119. In: Bökönyi, S. (ed.), *Cultural and Landscape Changes in South-East Hungary, I.* 301–311. Archaeolingua, Budapest.

TROGMAYER, O. 1965a

Röszke–Lúdvár. *Régészeti Füzetek* 18, 18.

TROGMAYER, O. 1965b
Röszke–Lúdvár. *Régészeti Füzetek* 19, 15.

VENCZEL, M. 1997
Amphibians and reptiles. In: Marinescu-Bîlcu et al. (eds.), *Archaeological researches at Borduşani–Popină (Ialomiţa county). Preliminary report 1993–1994*. 106–107. Muzeul Naţional de Istorie a României, Bucureşti.

VOINEA, V. 1997
Artifacts made from hard raw material of animal origin. In: Marinescu-Bîlcu et al. (eds.), *Archaeological researches at Borduşani–Popină (Ialomiţa county). Preliminary report 1993–1994*. 72–84. Bucureşti: Muzeul Naţional de Istorie a României.

VÖRÖS, I. 1980
Zoological and palaeoeconomical investigations on the archaeozoological material of the Early Neolithic Körös Culture. *Folia Archaeologica* 31, 35–61.

VÖRÖS, I. 1983
Lion remains from the Late Neolithic and Copper Age of the Carpathian Basin. *Folia Archaeologica* 34, 33–50.

VÖRÖS, I. 1986a
A szerencs–taktaföldvári késő neolit telep állatcsontleletei (Animal bone fossils of the Late Neolithic settlement in Szerencs–Taktaföldvár). *Natura Borsodiensis* 1, 98–124.

VÖRÖS, I. 1986b
Animal remains from the funeral ceremonies in the Middle Copper Age cemetery at Tiszavalk–Tetes. *Folia Archaeologica* 37, 75–97.

VÖRÖS, I. 1987
A tiszalúc–sarkadi rézkori település állatcsontleletei (Előzetes jelentés) (Animal remains from the Copper Age settlement at Tiszalúc–Sarkad [Preliminary report]). *Folia Archaeologica* 38, 121–127.

WHITTLE, A., BARTOSIEWICZ, L., BORIĆ, D., PETTIT, P. – RICHARD, M. 2002
In the beginning: new radiocarbon dates for the early Neolithic in northern Serbia and south-east Hungary. *Antaeus* 25, 63–117.

WHITTLE, A. BARTOSIEWICZ, L., BORIĆ, D., PETTIT, P. – RICHARD, M.
2005
   New radiocarbon dates for the early Neolithic in northern Serbia and southeast Hungary: some omissions and corrections. *Antaeus* 28, 347–355.

WHITTLE, A. 2007 (in press)
   The setting of Ecsegfalva and Körös culture site locations. In: Whittle, A. (ed.), *The Early Neolithic on the Great Hungarian Plain: investigations of the Körös culture site of Ecsegfalva 23, County Békés*. Archaeological Institute of the Hungarian Academy of Sciences, Budapest.

Appendices

Appendix 1. The classification of identified species

Class: Aves
Order: Gaviiformes
   Family: Gaviidae
      Genus: *Gavia*
         Species: *Gavia arctica* (Linnaeus, 1758)
Order: Podicipediformes
   Family: Podicipedidae
      Genus: *Tachybaptus*
         Species: *Tachybaptus ruficollis* (Pallas, 1764)
      Genus: *Podiceps*
         Species: *Podiceps cristatus* (Linnaeus, 1758)
                Podiceps auritus (Linnaeus, 1758)
                Podiceps nigricollis C. L. Brehm, 1831
Order: Pelecaniformes
   Family: Phalacrocoracidae
      Genus: *Phalacrocorax*
         Species: *Phalacrocorax carbo* (Linnaeus, 1758)
   Family: Pelecanidae
      Genus: *Pelecanus*
         Species: *Pelecanus onocrotalus* Linnaeus, 1758
Order: Ciconiiformes
   Family: Ardeidae
      Genus: *Botaurus*
         Species: *Botaurus stellaris* (Linnaeus, 1758)
      Genus: *Nycticorax*
         Species: *Nycticorax nycticorax* (Linnaeus, 1758)
      Genus: *Egretta*
         Species: *Egretta garzetta* (Linnaeus, 1766)
                Egretta alba (Linnaeus, 1758)
      Genus: *Ardea*
         Species: *Ardea cinerea* Linnaeus, 1758
                Ardea purpurea Linnaeus, 1766

Family: Ciconiidae
　Genus: *Ciconia*
　　Species: *Ciconia nigra* (Linnaeus, 1758)
　　　　　Ciconia ciconia (Linnaeus, 1758)
Family: Threskiornithidae
　Genus: *Plegadis*
　　Species: *Plegadis falcinellus* (Linnaeus, 1766)
　Genus: *Platalea*
　　Species: *Platalea leucorodia* Linnaeus, 1758

Order: Anseriformes
　Family: Anatidae
　　Genus: *Cygnus*
　　　Species: *Cygnus olor* (Gmelin, 1789)
　　　　　　Cygnus columbianus (Ord, 1815)
　　　　　　Cygnus cygnus (Linnaeus, 1758)
　　Genus: *Anser*
　　　Species: *Anser fabalis* (Latham, 1787)
　　　　　　Anser albifrons (Scopoli, 1769)
　　　　　　Anser erythropus (Linnaeus, 1758)
　　　　　　Anser anser (Linnaeus, 1758)
　　Genus: *Branta*
　　　Species: *Branta leucopsis* (Bechstein, 1803)
　　Genus: *Anas*
　　　Species: *Anas penelope* Linnaeus, 1758
　　　　　　Anas strepera Linnaeus, 1758
　　　　　　Anas crecca Linnaeus, 1758
　　　　　　Anas platyrhynchos Linnaeus, 1758
　　　　　　Anas acuta Linnaeus, 1758
　　　　　　Anas querquedula Linnaeus, 1758
　　　　　　Anas clypeata Linnaeus, 1758
　　Genus: *Aythya*
　　　Species: *Aythya ferina* (Linnaeus, 1758)
　　　　　　Aythya nyroca (Güldenstadt, 1770)
　　　　　　Aythya fuligula (Linnaeus, 1758)
　　　　　　Aythya marila (Linnaeus, 1761)
　　Genus: *Mergus*
　　　Species: *Mergus merganser* Linnaeus, 1758

Order: Accipitriformes
    Family: Accipitridae
        Genus: *Pernis*
            Species: *Pernis apivorus* (Linnaeus, 1758)
        Genus: *Haliaeetus*
            Species: *Haliaeetus albicilla* (Linnaeus, 1758)
        Genus: *Gypaetus*
            Species: *Gypaetus barbatus* (Linnaeus, 1758)
        Genus: *Circaetus*
            Species: *Circaetus gallicus* (Gmelin, 1788)
        Genus: *Circus*
            Species: *Circus aeruginosus* (Linnaeus, 1758)
                  Circus macrourus (Gmelin, 1771)
        Genus: *Accipiter*
            Species: *Accipiter gentilis* (Linnaeus, 1758)
        Genus: *Buteo*
            Species: *Buteo buteo* (Linnaeus, 1758)
        Genus: *Aquila*
            Species: *Aquila pomarina* C. L. Brehm, 1831
                  Aquila clanga Pallas, 1811
                  Aquila heliaca Savigny, 1809
                  Aquila chrysaetos (Linnaeus, 1758)
        Genus: *Hieraaetus*
            Species: *Hieraaetus pennatus* (Gmelin, 1788)
Order: Falconiformes
    Family: Falconidae
        Genus: *Falco*
            Species: *Falco peregrinus* Tunstall, 1771
Order: Galliformes
    Family: Tetraonidae
        Genus: *Tetrao*
            Species: *Tetrao tetrix* Linnaeus, 1758
    Family: Phasianidae
        Genus: *Perdix*
            Species: *Perdix perdix* (Linnaeus, 1758)

Order: Gruiformes
   Family: Rallidae
      Genus: *Porzana*
         Species: *Porzana porzana* (Linnaeus, 1766)
      Genus: *Gallinula*
         Species: *Gallinula chloropus* (Linnaeus, 1758)
      Genus: *Fulica*
         Species: *Fulica atra* Linnaeus, 1758
   Family: Gruidae
      Genus: *Grus*
         Species: *Grus grus* (Linnaeus, 1758)
      Genus: *Anthropoides*
         Species: *Anthropoides virgo* (Linnaeus, 1758)
   Family: Otitidae
      Genus: *Tetrax*
         Species: *Tetrax tetrax* (Linnaeus, 1758)
      Genus: *Otis*
         Species: *Otis tarda* Linnaeus, 1758

Order: Charadriiformes
   Family: Scolopacidae
      Genus: *Scolopax*
         Species: *Scolopax rusticola* Linnaeus, 1758
      Genus: *Limosa*
         Species: *Limosa limosa* (Linnaeus, 1758)
   Family: Laridae
      Genus: *Larus*
         Species: *Larus argentatus* Pontoppidan, 1763

Order: Columbiformes
   Family: Columbidae
      Genus: *Columba*
         Species: *Columba palumbus* Linnaeus, 1758

Order: Strigiformes
   Family: Strigidae
      Genus: *Bubo*
         Species: *Bubo bubo* (Linnaeus, 1758)

Genus: *Strix*
Species: *Strix aluco* Linnaeus, 1758
Genus: *Asio*
Species: *Asio flammeus* (Pontoppidan, 1763)
Order: Coraciiformes
Family: Coraciidae
Genus: *Coracias*
Species: *Coracias garrulus* Linnaeus, 1758
Family: Upupidae
Genus: *Upupa*
Species: *Upupa epops* Linnaeus, 1758
Order: Piciformes
Family: Picidae
Genus: *Dendrocopos*
Species: *Dendrocopos major* (Linnaeus, 1758)
Order: Passeriformes
Family: Alaudidae
Genus: *Alauda*
Species: *Alauda arvensis* Linnaeus, 1758
Family: Hirundinidae
Genus: *Riparia*
Species: *Riparia riparia* (Linnaeus, 1758)
Genus: *Hirundo*
Species: *Hirundo rustica* Linnaeus, 1758
Family: Turdidae
Genus: *Turdus*
Species: *Turdus merula* Linnaeus, 1758
Turdus pilaris Linnaeus, 1758
Turdus viscivorus Linnaeus, 1758
Family: Sylviidae
Genus: *Acrocephalus*
Family: Corvidae
Genus: *Garrulus*
Species: *Garrulus glandarius* (Linnaeus, 1758)
Genus: *Pica*
Species: *Pica pica* (Linnaeus, 1758)

        Genus: *Corvus*
            Species: *Corvus frugilegus* Linnaeus, 1758
                    Corvus corone Linnaeus, 1758
                    Corvus corax Linnaeus, 1758
Family: Sturnidae
    Genus: *Sturnus*
        Species: *Sturnus vulgaris* Linnaeus, 1758
Family: Passeridae
    Genus: *Passer*
        Species: *Passer domesticus* (Linnaeus, 1758)

Appendix 2. Measurements of avian remains
(mm; standard by von den Driesch 1976).
Abbreviations: GL – greatest length; SM – smallest length (Lm in coracoideum and femur, Dic in scapula, LC in sternum and LV in pelvis); Bp – proximal width (Dip in tibiotarsus); Dp – proximal depth (Dip in ulna); SC – smallest width of the diaphysis; Bd and Did – distal width (Bb in coracoideum); Dd – distal depth (BF in coracoideum); N – Neolithic; Ch – Chalcolithic.

Species	Skeletal Part	GL	SL	Bp	Dp	SC	Bd/Did	Dd	Site	Country	Age	Note
Podiceps ruficollis	tibiotarsus	65,8							Maroslele–Pana	Hungary	N	
Podiceps cristatus	coracoideum		37,1			3,7			Taşaul	Romania	Ch	
	humerus	94,2							Maroslele–Pana	Hungary	N	
	humerus	105,0		17,0			10,0		Tiszaluc–Sarkad	Hungary	Ch	
	humerus			18,8		6,0			Hârşova	Romania	Ch	
	ulna			7,8		3,4			Nagykörű Tsz.	Hungary	N	
	tibiotarsus			10,3					Endrőd 3/6	Hungary	N	
	tarsometatarsus					3,4	9,2	7,7	Isaccea	Romania	N	
Podiceps nigricollis	tibiotarsus					3,1	6,5	6,2	Taşaul	Romania	Ch	
Pelecanus onocrotalus	tibiotarsus					13,7	22,6	24,2	Isaccea	Romania	N	subadult
	ulna			36,2	38,2				Însurăţei	Romania	Ch	
Phalacrocorax carbo	coracoideum					5,9	30,7	24,5	Hârşova	Romania	Ch	
	scapula		18,3		7,7	6,9			Endrőd 3/6	Hungary	N	
	scapula		20,2			6,5			Taşaul	Romania	Ch	
	humerus			24,9					Borduşani–Popină	Romania	Ch	
	humerus			25,2					Hârşova	Romania	Ch	
	humerus			25,9					Hârşova	Romania	Ch	
	humerus			26,2					Hârşova	Romania	Ch	
	humerus					8,3	16,6	11,7	Hârşova	Romania	Ch	
	humerus					8,8	15,72	11,3	Hârşova	Romania	Ch	
	humerus					9,13			Hârşova	Romania	Ch	
	ulna			13,2		6,5			Hârşova	Romania	Ch	
	ulna			13,3	17,8	5,8			Borduşani–Popină	Romania	Ch	
	ulna					6,2	11,8	8,7	Borduşani–Popină	Romania	Ch	
	ulna					6,3	11,4	8,6	Borduşani–Popină	Romania	Ch	
	ulna					7,0	12,8	9,1	Vităneşti	Romania	Ch	
	radius			6,7	8,3	3,7			Borduşani–Popină	Romania	Ch	
	carpometacarpus	71,1		14,1		7,3	7,8	5,2	Borduşani–Popină	Romania	Ch	
	carpometacarpus	76,7					8,4	5,4	Hârşova	Romania	Ch	

Species	Skeletal Part	GL	SL	Bp	Dp	SC	Bd/Did	Dd	Site	Country	Age	Note
Phalacrocorax carbo	carpometacarpus	78,0		15,4		8,0	9,6	6,1	Hârşova	Romania	Ch	
	carpometacarpus	82,4		16,1		8,1	9,3	6	Borduşani–Popină	Romania	Ch	
	phalanx anterior 2/II			4,5	4,9				Taşaul	Romania	Ch	
	femur	62,4	60,3	18,4	13,2	7,8	17,8	11,5	Borduşani–Popină	Romania	Ch	
	femur	65,5	62	17,9	10,8	7,1	17,4	12,1	Endrőd 3/6	Hungary	N	subadult
	femur	66,9		18,2	11,4	8,3		12,2	Endrőd 3/6	Hungary	N	
	tibiotarsus	125,2		12,3	18,7	7,4	14,0	11,7	Hârşova	Romania	Ch	
	tibiotarsus					6,4	13,0	11,0	Căscioarele	Romania	Ch	
	tibiotarsus					7,1	11,2	10,0	Luncaviţa	Romania	Ch	
	tibiotarsus					7,1	11,6	9,0	Hârşova	Romania	Ch	
	tibiotarsus					7,1	13,1	11,0	Taşaul	Romania	Ch	
	tarsometatarsus	63,8			17,8	7,0			Taşaul	Romania	Ch	
	tarsometatarsus	65,8		14,8	18,3	7,4	16,0	9,5	Hârşova	Romania	Ch	
	tarsometatarsus			13,5		6,9			Endrőd 3/6	Hungary	N	
Phalacrocorax pygmeus	humerus					ap. 8,1	13,9	11,2	Borduşani–Popină	Romania	Ch	
Botaurus stellaris	carpometacarpus	64,5		14,6			9,5	6,8	Hârşova	Romania	Ch	
	carpometacarpus						7,5	5,4	Ecsegfalva 23	Hungary	N	
	ulna					6,4	10	8,7	Hârşova	Romania	Ch	
Nyctycorax nyctycorax	carpometacarpus						2,9		Ecsegfalva 23	Hungary	N	
	tibiotarsus					4,8	9,4	9,2	Hârşova	Romania	Ch	
	tibiotarsus					5,6	11,6	11,5	Tiszaszőlős–Domaháza	Hungary	N	
Egretta garzetta	carpometacarpus					2,6	6,6	4,4	Endrőd 3/6	Hungary	N	
Egretta alba	coracoideum		62,0			5,3			Nagykörű Tsz.	Hungary	N	
	coracoideum		62,1			6,0			Isaccea	Romania	N	
	coracoideum		64,4			5,1		20,2	Nagykörű Tsz.	Hungary	N	
	humerus			29,1		12,1			Isaccea	Romania	N	
	humerus					10,5	22,0	12,1	Nagykörű Tsz.	Hungary	N	
	carpometacarpus	85,0	81,2	17,3		10,4	10,7	7,4	Endrőd 3/6	Hungary	N	
	femur			13,2	10,2	6,5	14,3	12,4	Borduşani–Popină	Romania	Ch	
	tibiotarsus			11,6	15,6	6,1	11,9	12,3	Borduşani–Popină	Romania	Ch	
	tibiotarsus			11,7	15,3	6,1	11,8	13,1	Borduşani–Popină	Romania	Ch	
	tibiotarsus					7,0	8,8	11,7	Isaccea	Romania	N	
	tibiotarsus					7,3	13,4	14,7	Tiszaszőlős–Domaháza	Hungary	N	
	tibiotarsus						13,2	11,2	Hârşova	Romania	Ch	
	tarsometatarsus	125,7		13,0	13,4	5,8	13,9	8,6	Borduşani–Popină	Romania	Ch	

131

Species	Skeletal Part	GL	SL	Bp	Dp	SC	Bd/Did	Dd	Site	Country	Age	Note
Egretta alba	tarsometatarsus	126,5		12,9	13,6	5,8	13,3	8,6	Borduşani–Popină	Romania	Ch	
	tarsometatarsus			15,2					Ószentiván	Hungary	N	
	tarsometatarsus			15,7	18,5	7,0			Borduşani–Popină	Romania	Ch	
Ardea cinerea	coracoideum	63,5	58,0					17,0	Borduşani–Popină	Romania	Ch	
	coracoideum		60,8			5,8		19,5	Borduşani–Popină	Romania	Ch	
	coracoideum		58,8			5,7			Nagykörű Tsz.	Hungary	N	
	humerus			26,0					Endrőd 3/6	Hungary	N	
	humerus			28,3					Hârşova	Romania	Ch	
	humerus						19,0	9,5	Tiszaszőlős–Domaháza	Hungary	N	
	ulna			15,6	17,0				Borduşani–Popină	Romania	Ch	
	ulna					6,8	13,1	11,4	Borduşani–Popină	Romania	Ch	
	ulna					6,9	12,4	11,1	Hârşova	Romania	Ch	
	ulna						12,4	9,5	Căscioarele–Ostrovel	Romania	Ch	
	ulna						13,0	11,4	Borduşani–Popină	Romania	Ch	
	radius			7,9	6,4				Hârşova	Romania	Ch	
	radius					4,1	11,5	4,7	Hârşova	Romania	Ch	
	radius					4,5	11,7	4,8	Hârşova	Romania	Ch	
	radius					4,5	11,9	4,3	Hârşova	Romania	Ch	
	carpometacarpus	90,5				8,9	9,4	5,4	Nagykörű Tsz.	Hungary	N	
	carpometacarpus	98,5				9,8	10,1	6,8	Borduşani–Popină	Romania	Ch	
	carpometacarpus			ap. 15,0		8,4			Borduşani–Popină	Romania	Ch	
	carpometacarpus			15,5		9,6			Endrőd 3/6	Hungary	N	
	carpometacarpus			15,7					Endrőd 3/6	Hungary	N	
	carpometacarpus			16,5					Ecsegfalva 23	Hungary	N	
	carpometacarpus			16,7		9,1			Borduşani–Popină	Romania	Ch	
	carpometacarpus			17,1					Ecsegfalva 23	Hungary	N	
	carpometacarpus						9,6	6,0	Endrőd 3/6	Hungary	N	
	carpometacarpus						10,0		Röszke-Lúdvár	Hungary	N	
	carpometacarpus						10,1	6,7	Borduşani–Popină	Romania	Ch	
	carpometacarpus						10,3	6,8	Endrőd 3/6	Hungary	N	
	carpometacarpus						10,5	7,7	Ecsegfalva 23	Hungary	N	
	phalanx anterior 2/II	36,0				3,0			Röszke-Lúdvár	Hungary	N	

Species	Skeletal Part	GL	SL	Bp	Dp	SC	Bd/Did	Dd	Site	Country	Age	Note
Ardea cinerea	femur			15,0	8,8				Nagykörű Tsz.	Hungary	N	
	femur			15,8			15,5		Röszke-Lúdvár	Hungary	N	
	tibiotarsus			12,2					Borduşani–Popină	Romania	Ch	
	tibiotarsus					6,0	12,1	13,7	Nagykörű Tsz.	Hungary	N	
	tibiotarsus					6,9	12,8	12,8	Hârşova	Romania	Ch	
	tibiotarsus					7,8	12,7	12,8	Borduşani–Popină	Romania	Ch	
	tibiotarsus						12,0		Röszke-Lúdvár	Hungary	N	
	tibiotarsus						12,3	11,7	Hârşova	Romania	Ch	
	tarsometatarsus			13,0					Röszke-Lúdvár	Hungary	N	
	tarsometatarsus			13,5	16,8	6,4			Hârşova	Romania	Ch	
	tarsometatarsus					6,2	13,6	8,8	Hârşova	Romania	Ch	
	tarsometatarsus					6,2	13,9	7,8	Vităneşti	Romania	Ch	
Ardea purpurea	coracoideum		55,0						Röszke-Lúdvár	Hungary	N	
	humerus			20,6	7,6	6,8			Hârşova	Romania	Ch	
	humerus			22,0			17,0		Röszke-Lúdvár	Hungary	N	
	humerus					7,8	17,3	9,1	Borduşani–Popină	Romania	Ch	
	humerus					8,4	15,6	8,6	Hârşova	Romania	Ch	subadult
	ulna			11,4					Felsővadász–Várdomb	Hungary	N	
	ulna			14,1		6,8			Coslogeni	Romania	N	
	ulna					4,5	8,4	6,6	Hârşova	Romania	Ch	subadult
	ulna					5,0	10,3	9,1	Ecsegfalva 23	Hungary	N	
	radius			5,2	4,0	3,0			Hârşova	Romania	Ch	
	radius			5,6	4,7	3,3			Debrecen–Nyulas	Hungary	N	
	radius			6,0	5,8	3,9			Borduşani–Popină	Romania	Ch	
	radius			6,5	5,5	3,8			Ecsegfalva 23	Hungary	N	
	carpometacarpus	71,3		13,0			7,9	4,8	Hârşova	Romania	Ch	
	carpometacarpus	72,0		12,9		7,1	7,2	4,7	Borduşani–Popină	Romania	Ch	
	carpometacarpus			11,8	8,8				Borduşani–Popină	Romania	Ch	
	carpometacarpus			12,8	9,1				Ecsegfalva 23	Hungary	N	
	carpometacarpus			13,3					Hârşova	Romania	Ch	
	carpometacarpus			13,7	9,8	3,9			Ecsegfalva 23	Hungary	N	
	carpometacarpus					3,5	7,6	4,8	Ecsegfalva 23	Hungary	N	
	carpometacarpus						7,2		Röszke-Lúdvár	Hungary	N	

133

Species	Skeletal Part	GL	SL	Bp	Dp	SC	Bd/Did	Dd	Site	Country	Age	Note
Ardea purpurea	phalanx anterior 2/II	27,7		6,0	5,9			3,5	Ecsegfalva 23	Hungary	N	
Ciconia cf. *nigra*	humerus						30,5		Röszke–Lúdvár	Hungary	N	
Ciconia cf. *ciconia*	radius			8,1	7,0	4,9			Ciulniţa	Romania	N	
	carpometacarpus	102,0							Röszke–Lúdvár	Hungary	N	
	carpometacarpus			23,5					Endrőd 39	Hungary	N	
	femur						22,5		Röszke–Lúdvár	Hungary	N	
Platalea leucorodia	coracoideum		55,0						Tiszaluc–Sarkad	Hungary	Ch	
	ulna	160,0							Endrőd 39	Hungary	N	
	carpometacarpus	75,0		15,5				7,5	Ecsegfalva 23	Hungary	N	
	carpometacarpus	82,0							Tiszavasvári–Keresztfal	Hungary	N	
	phalanx anterior 2/II	35,8		7,6	6,2	10,6	7,6	4,6	Ecsegfalva 23	Hungary	N	
Plegadis falcinellus	coracoideum	40,7	37,5			5,3		14,7	Hârşova	Romania	Ch	
	ulna			10,7		4,8			Borduşani–Popină	Romania	Ch	
	radius					2,8	7,2	3,7	Borduşani–Popină	Romania	Ch	
	carpometacarpus			12,1		7,2	7,3	5,3	Borduşani–Popină	Romania	Ch	
	tibiotarsus						8,2	9,3	Hârşova	Romania	Ch	
Cygnus cf. *olor*	coracoideum	ap. 103,5	ap. 90,0			13,8		37,5	Hârşova	Romania	Ch	
	coracoideum						44,1	40,9	Taşaul	Romania	Ch	
	coracoideum		ap. 80,0			13,00			Borduşani–Popină	Romania	Ch	
	humerus			58,7					Endrőd 3/6	Hungary	N	
	humerus					ap. 17,9	38,5	19,6	Borduşani–Popină	Romania	Ch	
	humerus						33,8	21,4	Taşaul	Romania	Ch	
	humerus						37,0	20,0	Borduşani–Popină	Romania	Ch	
	ulna			24,5	28,4				Endrőd 3/6	Hungary	N	
	ulna					10,9	22,5	17,7	Borduşani–Popină	Romania	Ch	
	ulna					ap. 11,0	19,3	17,7	Borduşani–Popină	Romania	Ch	
	ulna					12,2	25,7	19,1	Borduşani–Popină	Romania	Ch	
	ulna						23,0	16,0	Endrőd 3/6	Hungary	N	
	radius			9,9	10,1				Isaccea	Romania	N	
	radius						19,7	9,4	Isaccea	Romania	N	

Species	Skeletal Part	GL	SL	Bp	Dp	SC	Bd/Did	Dd	Site	Country	Age	Note
Cygnus cf. olor	radius					7,6	ap. 14,0		Borduşani–Popină	Romania	Ch	
	carpometacarpus	133,0							Luncaviţa	Romania	Ch	
	carpometacarpus			32,4		7,7			Endrőd 3/6	Hungary	N	
	tibiotarsus			35,3					Borduşani–Popină	Romania	Ch	
	tibiotarsus			38,7					Endrőd 3/6	Hungary	N	
	tibiotarsus					12,6	23,8	22,2	Insurăţei	Romania	Ch	
	tibiotarsus					12,6	24,2	23,7	Borduşani–Popină	Romania	Ch	
Cygnus columbianus	scapula		24,7			9,7			Hârşova	Romania	Ch	
Cygnus cf. cygnus	scapula		31,7			12,6			Vităneşti	Romania	Ch	
	carpometacarpus	139,1		30,7		12,7	15,9	11,5	Vităneşti	Romania	Ch	
	carpometacarpus	141,0							Tiszaluc–Sarkad	Hungary	Ch	
	carpometacarpus	ap. 147,0				13,6			Căscioarele	Romania	Ch	
	carpometacarpus			31,0					Hârşova	Romania	Ch	
	carpometacarpus			31,5	20,8				Vităneşti	Romania	Ch	
	femur			32,0		12,7			Hârşova	Romania	Ch	male
	femur					14,2	30,3	19,0	Hârşova	Romania	Ch	
	tibiotarsus					12,1	25,2	25,7	Hârşova	Romania	Ch	male
	tarsometatarsus	127,8		27,2		11,1	27,5	21,3	Hârşova	Romania	Ch	
	tarsometatarsus			34,5					Hârşova	Romania	Ch	
	tarsometatarsus					ap. 10,0	28,5	22,4	Hârşova	Romania	Ch	male
	tarsometatarsus					11,0	28,7	22,5	Vităneşti	Romania	Ch	
Anser fabalis	carpometacarpus	85,5		20,4					Szolnok–Szanda	Hungary	N	
	carpometacarpus	86,0		19,0			10,5		Endrőd 39	Hungary	N	
Anser albifrons	humerus	144,0					22,2		Ószentiván	Hungary	N	
Anser anser	coracoideum	80,6	72,3			10,6		30,5	Căscioarele	Romania	Ch	
	coracoideum	84,6	75,0			10,7	35,5	33,2	Hârşova	Romania	Ch	
	scapula		16,7			8,6			Borduşani–Popină	Romania	Ch	
	scapula		18,7			8,7			Hârşova	Romania	Ch	
	scapula		20,2			9,6			Hârşova	Romania	Ch	
	scapula		20,7			7,9			Hârşova	Romania	Ch	
	scapula		21,1			7,5			Hârşova	Romania	Ch	
	scapula		21,6			8,4			Borduşani–Popină	Romania	Ch	
	scapula		21,7			8,6			Căscioarele	Romania	Ch	
	scapula		23,2			9,1			Hârşova	Romania	Ch	
	humerus	ap. 180,0				11,9	25,2	15,8	Nagykörű Tsz.	Hungary	N	

Species	Skeletal Part	GL	SL	Bp	Dp	SC	Bd/Did	Dd	Site	Country	Age	Note
Anser anser	humerus			38,4					Căscioarele	Romania	Ch	
	humerus			36,0		11,9			Hârşova	Romania	Ch	
	humerus					10,6	21,8	13,5	Căscioarele	Romania	Ch	
	humerus					11,8			Borduşani–Popină	Romania	Ch	
	humerus					12,1	25,7	14,6	Borduşani–Popină	Romania	Ch	
	humerus					12,5	27,6	14,7	Borduşani–Popină	Romania	Ch	
	humerus					12,6	25,0	15,0	Hârşova	Romania	Ch	
	humerus					12,6	26,8	15,4	Borduşani–Popină	Romania	Ch	
	humerus					14,1	27,3	16,2	Hârşova	Romania	Ch	male
	ulna			16,6	20,2				Tiszaszőlős–Domaháza	Hungary	N	
	ulna			16,8					Hârşova	Romania	Ch	
	ulna			16,8					Hârşova	Romania	Ch	
	ulna					9,2	17,1	12	Hârşova	Romania	Ch	
	ulna						17,7	11,5	Hârşova	Romania	Ch	
	ulna						18,1	13,3	Hârşova	Romania	Ch	
	radius	145,3				4,2			Borduşani–Popină	Romania	Ch	
	radius	145,3		9,2	8,1	4,1	10,9	4,9	Hârşova	Romania	Ch	
	radius	158,9		9,3	8,7	5,6	11,7	6	Borduşani–Popină	Romania	Ch	
	radius			8,6	7,8	4,6			Hârşova	Romania	Ch	
	radius			8,7	8,1	6,4			Borduşani–Popină	Romania	Ch	
	radius			8,7	10,1	5,0			Isaccea	Romania	N	
	radius						10,7	5,4	Insurăţei	Romania	Ch	
	radius			9,0	8,2				Hârşova	Romania	Ch	
	radius			9,3	7,7	5			Hârşova	Romania	Ch	
	radius			9,1	7,6	5,7			Hârşova	Romania	Ch	
	radius					4,2	11,6	6,2	Hârşova	Romania	Ch	male
	radius					4,3	10,2	5,2	Hârşova	Romania	Ch	
	radius					ap. 4,5	10,8	5,2	Hârşova	Romania	Ch	subadult
	radius						10,8	5,3	Hârşova	Romania	Ch	
	radius						11,6	5,8	Hârşova	Romania	Ch	
	carpometacarpus	95,9		21,4		10,8	11,7	8,0	Hârşova	Romania	Ch	
	carpometacarpus	97,9		20,6		11,0	11,0	7,2	Borduşani–Popină	Romania	Ch	
	carpometacarpus	98,5							Szolnok–Szanda	Hungary	N	
	carpometacarpus	100,4				10,3	11,2	8,4	Hârşova	Romania	Ch	

Species	Skeletal Part	GL	SL	Bp	Dp	SC	Bd/Did	Dd	Site	Country	Age	Note
Anser anser	carpometacarpus	101,2		24,0					Szolnok–Szanda	Hungary	N	
	carpometacarpus	101,4		25,3		11,0	12,4	8,1	Hârşova	Romania	Ch	male
	carpometacarpus	101,7		24,7			11,0	8,4	Hârşova	Romania	Ch	
	carpometacarpus	102,0							Endrőd 39	Hungary	N	
	carpometacarpus	104,1		24,7		10,4	12,3	8,3	Hârşova	Romania	Ch	
	carpometacarpus			21,0					Hârşova	Romania	Ch	
	carpometacarpus			22,7					Ciulniţa	Romania	N	
	carpometacarpus			24,4					Hârşova	Romania	Ch	
	carpometacarpus						11,5	7,7	Hârşova	Romania	Ch	
	carpometacarpus						11,7	7,7	Hârşova	Romania	Ch	
	phalanx anterior 1/II	45,5		10,5	8,5	12,6	11,4	6,2	Hârşova	Romania	Ch	
	phalanx anterior 1/II			9,0	8,2	11,7			Ciulniţa	Romania	N	
	femur	79,8	75,4	18,4		7,4	18,6	13,7	Borduşani–Popină	Romania	Ch	
	femur	89,7	84,6	21,7	15,2	8,9	20,8	17,0	Hârşova	Romania	Ch	
	tibiotarsus			22,7		8,2			Nagykörű Tsz.	Hungary	N	
	tibiotarsus					6,2	13,9	14,7	Hârşova	Romania	Ch	
	tarsometatarsus	ap. 80,0		17,6	16,2	7,30	18,0	ap. 13,0	Borduşani–Popină	Romania	Ch	
	tarsometatarsus			17,0					Hârşova	Romania	Ch	
	tarsometatarsus					7,5	19,1	13,1	Hârşova	Romania	Ch	
	tarsometatarsus					8,8	18,4	8,0	Borduşani–Popină	Romania	Ch	
	tarsometatarsus						20,1	14,7	Hârşova	Romania	Ch	
Branta leucopsis	carpometacarpus	79,6		19,5		9,3	10,1	7,4	Nagykörű Tsz.	Hungary	N	
Mergus cf. merganser	tibiotarsus					4,9	9,7	9,7	Ecsegfalva 23	Hungary	N	
Anas crecca	coracoideum	34,5	33,4	4,5	5,2	3,5		10,7	Endrőd 3/6	Hungary	N	
	coracoideum	38,4	36,0	5,5/3,7	6,1	3,9		14,8	Endrőd 3/6	Hungary	N	
	coracoideum					3,6		11,4	Endrőd 3/6	Hungary	N	
	coracoideum							10,9	Ecsegfalva 23	Hungary	N	
	scapula		6,9			2,6			Ecsegfalva 23	Hungary	N	
	scapula		8,1			2,7			Ecsegfalva 23	Hungary	N	
	humerus	ap. 59,0				4,4	9,3	5,5	Endrőd 3/6	Hungary	N	
	humerus	59,7		13,6		4,8	9,0	5,7	Vităneşti	Romania	Ch	male
	ulna			6,7	7,9	3,6			Ecsegfalva 23	Hungary	N	
	ulna					3,2	6,6	5,4	Ecsegfalva 23	Hungary	N	
	carpometacarpus	36,5	33,9	8,6	5,3	2,8	4,6	3,2	Ecsegfalva 23	Hungary	N	
	tarsometatarsus	30,5		6,4	6,5	3,4	6,5	5,2	Borduşani–Popină	Romania	Ch	

137

Species	Skeletal Part	GL	SL	Bp	Dp	SC	Bd/Did	Dd	Site	Country	Age	Note
Anas penelope	coracoideum	42,0	39,2			4,9		15,8	Tiszaszőlős–Domaháza	Hungary	N	
	humerus	ap. 73,0				5,9			Tiszaszőlős–Domaháza	Hungary	N	
	humerus	75,5		16,5			12,0		Endrőd 39	Hungary	N	
	carpometacarpus			11,6		7,0			Coslogeni	Romania	N	
	carpometacarpus						6,7	5,0	Borduşani–Popină	Romania	Ch	
Anas cf. clypeata	coracoideum	45,3		6,2		4,5		16,1	Endrőd 3/6	Hungary	N	
	coracoideum	45,6		6,9		4,7	19,0	18,2	Endrőd 3/6	Hungary	N	
	humerus			18,3		7,0			Endrőd 3/6	Hungary	N	
	humerus					6,1	12,9	7,6	Endrőd 3/6	Hungary	N	
	ulna	ap. 65,0		7,7		4,2	8,4	5,3	Endrőd 3/6	Hungary	N	
	ulna			7,4		4,2			Endrőd 3/6	Hungary	N	
	carpometacarpus	47,8		11,0			5,5	4,2	Endrőd 3/6	Hungary	N	
	tibiotarsus					3,8	6,8	7,5	Hârşova	Romania	Ch	
Anas querquedula	coracoideum							14,7	Ecsegfalva 23	Hungary	N	
	scapula		8,9			3,3			Ecsegfalva 23	Hungary	N	
	humerus	64,0		14,4		4,7	9,4	5,8	Borduşani Popina	Romania	Ch	
	humerus					4,9	10,0	6,0	Endrőd 3/6	Hungary	N	
	ulna		6,2	6,9	8,6				Ecsegfalva 23	Hungary	N	
	ulna			6,2		3,3			Endrőd 3/6	Hungary	N	
	ulna			7,2	3,4	3,4			Ecsegfalva 23	Hungary	N	
	ulna					3,5	6,3	5,9	Ecsegfalva 23	Hungary	N	
	radius	52,5		3,9	3,5	2,2	4,5	2,8	Borduşani Popina	Romania	Ch	
	carpometacarpus	42,6	39,5	9,9	5,9	3,3	5,8	3,9	Ecsegfalva 23	Hungary	N	
Anas acuta	coracoideum					4,5		16,9	Ecsegfalva 23	Hungary	N	
	humerus					5,1	10,5	7,3	Luncaviţa	Romania	Ch	
	ulna				7,5	5,2			Borduşani–Popină	Romania	Ch	
	radius			3,7	4,2	2,2			Taşaul	Romania	Ch	
	radius			5,1	4,2				Ecsegfalva 23	Hungary	N	
	carpometacarpus	52,1		11,7	6,9	6,9	7,9	4,9	Borduşani–Popină	Romania	Ch	
	carpometacarpus	53,4		12,1	7,7		6,9	4,8	Ecsegfalva 23	Hungary	N	
Anas platyrhynchos	coracoideum	54,7							Maroslele–Pana	Hungary	N	
	coracoideum	55,2	51,1			6,0		20,3	Ecsegfalva 23	Hungary	N	
	coracoideum	55,9	50,6			5,8		21,2	Borduşani–Popină	Romania	Ch	
	coracoideum	57,1	51,9			5,9		21,9	Borduşani–Popină	Romania	Ch	
	coracoideum	57,8	53,2			6,0	23,0	20,9	Endrőd 3/6	Hungary	N	

Species	Skeletal Part	GL	SL	Bp	Dp	SC	Bd/Did	Dd	Site	Country	Age	Note
Anas platyrhynchos	coracoideum	ap. 58,0	ap. 54,0			6,1	22,2	21,0	Tiszaszőlős–Domaháza	Hungary	N	
	coracoideum					4,8	21,4	19,8	Borduşani–Popină	Romania	Ch	
	coracoideum							18,4	Ecsegfalva 23	Hungary	N	
	coracoideum							20,5	Vităneşti	Romania	Ch	
	scapula		11,9						Borduşani–Popină	Romania	Ch	
	scapula		12,5						Borduşani–Popină	Romania	Ch	
	scapula		12,6			4,8			Tiszaszőlős–Domaháza	Hungary	N	
	scapula		12,9			4,7			Ecsegfalva 23	Hungary	N	
	scapula		12,9			5,5			Insurăţei	Romania	Ch	
	scapula		13,1			5,5			Endrőd 3/6	Hungary	N	
	scapula		13,2			4,8			Ecsegfalva 23	Hungary	N	
	humerus	92,0		20,8		7,0	14,2	9,1	Căscioarele	Romania	Ch	
	humerus	94,0		20,9		7,0	14,6	8,8	Borduşani–Popină	Romania	Ch	
	humerus	94,2							Maroslele–Pana	Hungary	N	
	humerus	94,2		20,9		7,4	14,6	8,9	Borduşani–Popină	Romania	Ch	
	humerus	95,0							Endrőd 39	Hungary	N	
	humerus	95,0		21,8		7,6	14,9	7,1	Endrőd 3/6	Hungary	N	
	humerus	97,0							Szajol–Felsőföld	Hungary	N	
	humerus	100,0							Szolnok–Szanda	Hungary	N	
	humerus			19,9		6,6			Endrőd 6	Hungary	N	
	humerus			20,4		6,6			Endrőd 6	Hungary	N	
	humerus			21,1		6,6			Nagykörű Tsz.	Hungary	N	
	humerus			21,4					Vităneşti	Romania	Ch	
	humerus			21,7		7,4			Endrőd 3/6	Hungary	N	
	humerus			21,9					Vităneşti	Romania	Ch	
	humerus			22,2					Tiszaszőlős–Domaháza	Hungary	N	
	humerus					6,6	11,5		Ecsegfalva 23	Hungary	N	
	humerus					6,6	13,1	7,9	Borduşani–Popină	Romania	Ch	
	humerus					6,7	13,4	10,1	Borduşani–Popină	Romania	Ch	
	humerus					6,8			Ecsegfalva 23	Hungary	N	
	humerus					6,9	14,0		Ecsegfalva 23	Hungary	N	
	humerus					7,1	14,6	8,5	Borduşani–Popină	Romania	Ch	
	humerus					7,2	14,4	8,3	Endrőd 3/6	Hungary	N	

Species	Skeletal Part	GL	SL	Bp	Dp	SC	Bd/Did	Dd	Site	Country	Age	Note
Anas platyrhynchos	humerus					7,3	15,0	9,0	Vităneşti	Romania	Ch	
	humerus					7,3	15,3	8,5	Endrőd 3/6	Hungary	N	
	humerus					7,3			Endrőd 3/6	Hungary	N	
	humerus					7,4	14,8	9,0	Endrőd 3/6	Hungary	N	
	humerus					7,5	14,5	8,8	Borduşani–Popină	Romania	Ch	
	humerus					7,5	14,7	8,8	Endrőd 3/6	Hungary	N	
	humerus					7,5	14,7	8,9	Endrőd 3/6	Hungary	N	
	humerus					7,6	14,3	8,6	Borduşani–Popină	Romania	Ch	
	humerus					7,6	15,4	9,1	Endrőd 3/6	Hungary	N	
	humerus						15,1	8,8	Vităneşti	Romania	Ch	
	ulna	ap. 73,0				5,0	10,0	6,6	Endrőd 3/6	Hungary	N	
	ulna	ap. 73,0				5,5	10,2	6,9	Endrőd 3/6	Hungary	N	
	ulna	73,1		9,5	12,2	4,9	10,1	8,5	Vităneşti	Romania	Ch	
	ulna	75,2		9,8	12,4	5,4	10,0	8,5	Vităneşti	Romania	Ch	
	ulna	77,4		9,7	12,2	5,4	10,3	6,7	Borduşani–Popină	Romania	Ch	
	ulna	79,7		10,0	12,6	5,4	10,1	8,7	Ciulniţa	Romania	N	
	ulna	ap. 80,0		10,2		5,5	10,3	6,9	Endrőd 3/6	Hungary	N	
	ulna	ap. 80,0		10,4		5,8	10,6	6,9	Endrőd 3/6	Hungary	N	
	ulna	80,1		9,9	12,6	5,6	10,3	8,7	Borduşani–Popină	Romania	Ch	
	ulna	80,3		10,1	12,9	5,7	10,4	8,9	Borduşani–Popină	Romania	Ch	
	ulna	81,0							Röszke–Lúdvár	Hungary	N	
	ulna			10,2		5,9			Endrőd 3/6	Hungary	N	
	ulna					4,6	9,8	8,2	Nagykörű Tsz.	Hungary	N	
	ulna					5,1	10,6	7,9	Ecsegfalva 23	Hungary	N	
	ulna					5,2			Ecsegfalva 23	Hungary	N	
	ulna					5,3	10,7	8,7	Endrőd 3/6	Hungary	N	
	ulna					5,4	10,8	7,0	Endrőd 3/6	Hungary	N	
	ulna					5,6	10,6	8,7	Ecsegfalva 23	Hungary	N	
	ulna					5,7	9,4	8,6	Borduşani–Popină	Romania	Ch	
	ulna						10,3	8,6	Ecsegfalva 23	Hungary	N	
	radius	74,2		5,5	4,8	3,4	6,7	4,0	Borduşani–Popină	Romania	Ch	
	radius			5,0	5,8	3,1			Endrőd 3/6	Hungary	N	
	radius			5,1	5,6	3,2			Endrőd 3/6	Hungary	N	
	radius					2,7		3,8	Hârşova tell	Romania	Ch	

Species	Skeletal Part	GL	SL	Bp	Dp	SC	Bd/Did	Dd	Site	Country	Age	Note
Anas platyrhynchos	radius					3,1	6,5	4,4	Endrőd 3/6	Hungary	N	
	radius					3,2	7,0	4,0	Coslogeni	Romania	N	
	radius					3,7	7,0	4,6	Endrőd 3/6	Hungary	N	
	carpometacarpus	52,6		12,7		7,9	7,0	4,9	Vităneşti	Romania	Ch	
	carpometacarpus	53,9		12,6			7,5	5,1	Borduşani–Popină	Romania	Ch	
	carpometacarpus	55,0					6,6	5,0	Ecsegfalva 23	Hungary	N	
	carpometacarpus	55,7		12,8			7,3	4,9	Ecsegfalva 23	Hungary	N	
	carpometacarpus	55,9							Szolnok–Szanda	Hungary	N	
	carpometacarpus	56,1				8,1	7,2	5,2	Ecsegfalva 23	Hungary	N	
	carpometacarpus	56,5							Szolnok–Szanda	Hungary	N	
	carpometacarpus	57,1							Szolnok–Szanda	Hungary	N	
	carpometacarpus	59,0		13,4		7,2	6,9	5,1	Borduşani–Popină	Romania	Ch	
	carpometacarpus	59,4		13,4		8,4	7,1	5,0	Borduşani–Popină	Romania	Ch	
	carpometacarpus	59,6		13,9					Ecsegfalva 23	Hungary	N	
	carpometacarpus	60,4		13,7			8,1	5,4	Ecsegfalva 23	Hungary	N	
	carpometacarpus	60,6		14,2			7,7	5,7	Ecsegfalva 23	Hungary	N	
	carpometacarpus	61,0		13,8			8,6	5,8	Ecsegfalva 23	Hungary	N	
	carpometacarpus	61,2		13,8			7,6	5,5	Endrőd 3/6	Hungary	N	
	carpometacarpus			12,7		8,0			Endrőd 3/6	Hungary	N	
	carpometacarpus			13,1					Ecsegfalva 23	Hungary	N	
	carpometacarpus			13,8		8,7			Borduşani–Popină	Romania	Ch	
	carpometacarpus						6,9	4,8	Ecsegfalva 23	Hungary	N	
	carpometacarpus						6,9	4,9	Endrőd 3/6	Hungary	N	
	carpometacarpus						7,0	4,9	Ecsegfalva 23	Hungary	N	
	carpometacarpus						7,7	5,6	Ecsegfalva 23	Hungary	N	
	phalanx anterior 1/II	21,9		6,0	5,1	7,3	6,2	4,1	Ecsegfalva 23	Hungary	N	
	phalanx anterior 1/II	23,9		6,3	4,8	7,4	6,3	3,7	Ecsegfalva 23	Hungary	N	
	femur	49,3	46,8	14,4	8,3	4,4	11,3	8,8	Endrőd 3/6	Hungary	N	
	femur	51,7	48,8	11,0	10,0	4,6	11,3	8,9	Borduşani–Popină	Romania	Ch	
	femur	51,7				4,3	11,6	7,9	Endrőd 3/6	Hungary	N	
	femur			11,2	7,1	4,7			Taşaul	Romania	Ch	
	femur			12,0	9,0				Endrőd 3/6	Hungary	N	
	femur			12,0	10,0	5,3			Borduşani–Popină	Romania	Ch	
	femur			12,1	8,5	4,6			Endrőd 3/6	Hungary	N	

Species	Skeletal Part	GL	SL	Bp	Dp	SC	Bd/Did	Dd	Site	Country	Age	Note
Anas platyrhynchos	femur					4,6	11,0	8,8	Borduşani–Popină	Romania	Ch	
	tibiotarsus	86,6		15,7		4,9	9,1	8,8	Borduşani–Popină	Romania	Ch	
	tibiotarsus	87,5		15,1		4,9	9,1	8,7	Borduşani–Popină	Romania	Ch	
	tibiotarsus			13,5					Endrőd 3/6	Hungary	N	
	tibiotarsus					4,0	8,5	8,0	Ecsegfalva 23	Hungary	N	
	tibiotarsus					4,2			Vităneşti	Romania	Ch	
	tibiotarsus					4,6	9,6	8,9	Endrőd 3/6	Hungary	N	
	tarsometatarsus	44,8		9,7	9,1	4,4	9,6	7,1	Ecsegfalva 23	Hungary	N	
	tarsometatarsus	45,7		9,4	9,1	4,4	9,9	8,1	Borduşani–Popină	Romania	Ch	
	tarsometatarsus	45,7		9,5		4,4	9,1	7,5	Borduşani–Popină	Romania	Ch	
	tarsometatarsus			9,7		5,5			Ecsegfalva 23	Hungary	N	
Anas cf. strepera	coracoideum	47,4	42,7	6,8	7,0	5,2		19,3	Ecsegfalva 23	Hungary	N	
	coracoideum					4,6		16,6	Ecsegfalva 23	Hungary	N	
	coracoideum					5,3		19,0	Ecsegfalva 23	Hungary	N	
	scapula		9,9			4,3			Ecsegfalva 23	Hungary	N	
	carpometacarpus	50,6		12,5		7,4	6,9	4,8	Taşaul	Romania	Ch	
	carpometacarpus	51,0		12,0			7,3	4,8	Ecsegfalva 23	Hungary	N	
	carpometacarpus			12,5					Ecsegfalva 23	Hungary	N	
Aythya cf. ferina	humerus	85,2							Maroslele–Pana	Hungary	N	
	humerus					5,7	12,2	7,5	Ecsegfalva 23	Hungary	N	
	ulna			7,9		4,0	8,4	6,8	Ecsegfalva 23	Hungary	N	
	carpometacarpus						5,8	3,9	Ecsegfalva 23	Hungary	N	
	femur			11,0		4,6			Endrőd 3/6	Hungary	N	
	tibiotarsus					3,5	8,5		Nagykörű Tsz.	Hungary	N	
Aythya nyroca	coracoideum		39,0			3,9			Ecsegfalva 23	Hungary	N	
	humerus	72,0		16,4		2,6			Ecsegfalva 23	Hungary	N	
	humerus			15,5		5,1			Ecsegfalva 23	Hungary	N	
	humerus					4,6	8,4	5,5	Ecsegfalva 23	Hungary	N	
	humerus					4,8	10,1	6,0	Endrőd 3/6	Hungary	N	
	humerus					4,9	9,8	6,1	Borduşani–Popină	Romania	Ch	
	humerus						10,0		Röszke–Lúdvár	Hungary	N	
	ulna	61,6	6,0	6,7	8,7	3,9			Ecsegfalva 23	Hungary	N	
	ulna					3,2	6,5	5,7	Ecsegfalva 23	Hungary	N	
	ulna						8,4	6,9	Ecsegfalva 23	Hungary	N	
	radius			4,1	3,3	2,2			Ecsegfalva 23	Hungary	N	
	radius			4,2	3,9	2,5			Ecsegfalva 23	Hungary	N	
	radius					2,1	4,4	2,7	Ecsegfalva 23	Hungary	N	
	carpometacarpus	37,5				2,6	4,9	3,3	Ecsegfalva 23	Hungary	N	

Species	Skeletal Part	GL	SL	Bp	Dp	SC	Bd/Did	Dd	Site	Country	Age	Note
Aythya nyroca	carpometacarpus	38,2		8,9		3,0	5,1	3,6	Ecsegfalva 23	Hungary	N	
	carpometacarpus	40,0		9,0					Tiszaszőlős–Domaháza	Hungary	N	
	tibiotarsus					3,1	6,7		Ecsegfalva 23	Hungary	N	
	tarsometatarsus			7,0		4,1			Ecsegfalva 23	Hungary	N	
Aythya fuligula	coracoideum	45,1	42,4				4,4	17,9	Taşaul	Romania	Ch	
	humerus			17,2		5,2			Ecsegfalva 23	Hungary	N	
	ulna						8,4	7,0	Ecsegfalva 23	Hungary	N	
Aythya marila	ulna	ap. 75				4,2	8,6	5,4	Tiszaszőlős–Domaháza	Hungary	N	
Pernis apivorus	radius	109,6		6,2	4,3	3,2	7,7	4,8	Hârşova	Romania	Ch	
Gypaetus barbatus	carpometacarpus	120,4					17,7	13,0	Vităneşti	Romania	Ch	
Haliaeetus albicilla	coracoideum	ap. 82,0				13,9			Borduşani–Popină	Romania	Ch	
	humerus						34,0		Berettyó-szentmárton	Hungary	N	male
	humerus						36,3		Insurăţei	Romania	Ch	female
	ulna			20,4	24,3				Hârşova	Romania	Ch	
	carpometacarpus	109,5		25,0					Szolnok–Szanda	Hungary	N	male
	carpometacarpus	112,0		25,8					Tiszaluc–Sarkad	Hungary	Ch	male
	carpometacarpus	115,1					15,2	12,2	Căscioarele	Romania	Ch	male
	carpometacarpus	123,0		27,6					Tiszaluc–Sarkad	Hungary	Ch	female
	carpometacarpus	124,3		28,1			20,9		Borduşani–Popină	Romania	Ch	female
	carpometacarpus						17,5	12,7	Hârşova	Romania	Ch	
	phalanx anterior 1/II	45,5		9,6	11,4	13,2		7,2	Borduşani–Popină	Romania	Ch	
	phalanx anterior 1/II	48,0				15,2			Tiszaluc–Sarkad	Hungary	Ch	
Circaetus gallicus	tibiotarsus					ap. 14-15			Röszke–Lúdvár	Hungary	N	
Circus macrourus	carpometacarpus			13,9					Vităneşti	Romania	Ch	
Accipiter gentilis	humerus					8,6	17,2	9,1	Hârşova	Romania	Ch	
	ulna	115,5	9,8	11,4	12,7	5,8	9,4	7,6	Hârşova	Romania	Ch	female
	ulna			10,3					Luncaviţa	Romania	Ch	
	carpometacarpus	56,2					8,5	5,9	Mezőzombor–Temető	Hungary	Ch	male
	femur					8,0	16,8	12,8	Ciulniţa	Romania	N	female
Buteo buteo	carpometacarpus	56,4	52,4	14,2	8,3	8,41	10,1	6,6	Hârşova	Romania	Ch	male
	carpometacarpus	58,1	54,7	13,5	5,5		8,7	6,4	Hârşova	Romania	Ch	male
	tarsometatarsus			11,8	9,3				Ecsegfalva 23	Hungary	N	male

143

Species	Skeletal Part	GL	SL	Bp	Dp	SC	Bd/Did	Dd	Site	Country	Age	Note
Aquila pomarina	coracoideum					7,7		ap. 20,6	Hârşova tell	Romania	Ch	
	ulna					7,2	12,1	9,0	Căscioarele	Romania	Ch	
	tibiotarsus						15,4	11,0	Tiszaszőlős–Domaháza	Hungary	N	female
Aquila heliaca	femur			23,6	17,1	11,4			Borduşani–Popină	Romania	Ch	
	radius						6,0	10,7	7,6 Hârşova	Romania	Ch	
Aquila chrysaetos	ph p. 3/II	38,0							Isaccea	Romania	N	
Hieraaetus pennatus	ulna					5,7	11,0	8,8	Căscioarele	Romania	Ch	
	carpometacarpus	58,0		13,3			8,5	6,5	Borduşani Popina	Romania	Ch	
	carpometacarpus	58,8		13,5		9,2	10,1	6,4	Hârşova	Romania	Ch	
	tarsometatarsus			10,9					Ecsegfalva 23	Hungary	N	
Pandion haliaaetus	femur	73,5	71,7	16	10,8	7,1	14,2	12,3	Borduşani–Popină	Romania	Ch	
	tarsometatarsus							16,3	Hârşova	Romania	Ch	
Falco peregrinus	femur	ap. 64,0	60,8			5,7			Vităneşti	Romania	Ch	male
Tetrao tetrix	coracoideum	62,8	59,8			4,8		15,9	Vităneşti	Romania	Ch	male
	scapula		15,5			6,7			Vităneşti	Romania	Ch	male
	humerus	79,0		21,6		7,3	14,8	8,6	Însurăţei	Romania	Ch	
	humerus			23,8					Vităneşti	Romania	Ch	male
	humerus			24,1					Vităneşti	Romania	Ch	male
	humerus			24,1					Vităneşti	Romania	Ch	male
	humerus					8,1	16,7	9,5	Vităneşti	Romania	Ch	male
	ulna	83,8		10,8	14,9	5,1	10,7	8,7	Ciulniţa	Romania	N	male
	ulna			8,4		4,4			Coslogeni	Romania	N	
	ulna					4,7	11,0	7,6	Vităneşti	Romania	Ch	male
	ulna						11,0	7,4	Vităneşti	Romania	Ch	male
	radius	69,3		4,9	5,5	2,8	6,7	3,5	Însurăţei	Romania	Ch	
	carpometacarpus	43,5		12,0		8,6	8,5	4,7	Coslogeni	Romania	N	
	carpometacarpus	47,7		13,8		9,5	9,8	5,6	Ecsegfalva 23	Hungary	N	male
	carpometacarpus	47,7				8,9		5,0	Vităneşti	Romania	Ch	male
	carpometacarpus	49,4		13,7		10,1	9,7	5,6	Vităneşti	Romania	Ch	maleale
	femur	84,8	80,5	16,3	10,4	6	14,7	11,7	Borduşani–Popină	Romania	Ch	male
	femur			16,2	10,5	6,7			Ecsegfalva 23	Hungary	N	male
	femur					6,7	14,7	11,1	Vităneşti	Romania	Ch	male
	tibiotarsus			18,2		5,4			Vităneşti	Romania	Ch	male
	tibiotarsus					5,3	8,8	ap. 8,9	Borduşani–Popină	Romania	Ch	male
	tibiotarsus					5,4	9,9	8,7	Borduşani–Popină	Romania	Ch	male
	tibiotarsus					5,5	9,5	9,0	Vităneşti	Romania	Ch	male

Species	Skeletal Part	GL	SL	Bp	Dp	SC	Bd/Did	Dd	Site	Country	Age	Note
Tetrao tetrix	tibiotarsus					5,7	10,0	9,9	Vităneşti	Romania	Ch	male
	tarsometatarsus	54,8		11,1	9,5	4,7			Vităneşti	Romania	Ch	male
Perdix perdix	ulna	45,4				2,4			Borduşani–Popină	Romania	Ch	juvenile
	ulna			4,4					Hârşova	Romania	Ch	
Porzana porzana	humerus					2,4	5,1	3,1	Ecsegfalva 23	Hungary	N	
	tibiotarsus						4,0	4,1	Hârşova	Romania	Ch	
Gallinula chloropus	scapula		7,0						Hârşova	Romania	Ch	
	humerus					3,5	7,4	4,2	Tiszaszőlős–Domaháza	Hungary	N	
	humerus						7,7	4,4	Hârşova	Romania	Ch	
	ulna	43,3		5,4	7,0	2,8	4,9	3,6	Hârşova	Romania	Ch	
Fulica atra	coracoideum	35,0	33,4			4,3	13,0	11,3	Tiszaszőlős–Domaháza	Hungary	N	
	scapula		9,4			3,6			Taşaul	Romania	Ch	
	humerus	72,0							Endrőd 39	Hungary	N	
	humerus	77,1		14,8		4,5	10,0	5,9	Hârşova	Romania	Ch	
	humerus			14,3					Tiszaszőlős–Domaháza	Hungary	N	
	humerus			14,5					Tiszavalk–Négyesi-határ	Hungary	N	
	humerus					4,3	9,9	6,1	Borduşani–Popină	Romania	Ch	
	humerus					4,4	9,5	5,6	Nagykörű Tsz.	Hungary	N	
	humerus					4,6	9,4	6,3	Borduşani–Popină	Romania	Ch	
	humerus					4,6	10,6	6,3	Tiszaszőlős–Domaháza	Hungary	N	
	humerus					4,7	9,3	5,3	Ecsegfalva 23	Hungary	N	
	humerus						9,4	5,3	Tiszaszőlős–Domaháza	Hungary	N	
	ulna	63,1		6,8	7,8	3,5	6,1	5,4	Ecsegfalva 23	Hungary	N	
	ulna				6,8	6,2			Borduşani–Popină	Romania	Ch	
	ulna					3,2	5,6	5,3	Ecsegfalva 23	Hungary	N	
	ulna					3,2	6,2	5,5	Endrőd 3/6	Hungary	N	
	ulna					3,9	5,9	6,0	Borduşani–Popină	Romania	Ch	
	radius	59,0		2,9	3,4	2,1	4,2	2,6	Ecsegfalva 23	Hungary	N	
	radius			3,2	3,9	2,3			Ecsegfalva 23	Hungary	N	
	radius					2,2	4,4	2,9	Ecsegfalva 23	Hungary	N	
	femur	57,5							Maroslele–Pana	Hungary	N	
	femur					4,0	9,6	7,4	Ecsegfalva 23	Hungary	N	
	tibiotarsus			11,0		4,0			Nagykörű Tsz.	Hungary	N	
	tibiotarsus					4,0	8,5	7,9	Ecsegfalva 23	Hungary	N	

Species	Skeletal Part	GL	SL	Bp	Dp	SC	Bd/Did	Dd	Site	Country	Age	Note
Fulica atra	tibiotarsus					4,1	8,7	8,3	Borduşani–Popină	Romania	Ch	
	tibiotarsus					4,2	9,2	8,8	Borduşani–Popină	Romania	Ch	
	tibiotarsus							8,8	Ószentiván	Hungary	N	
	tibiotarsus							9,0	Röszke–Lúdvár	Hungary	N	
	tarsometatarsus	55,6		9,3	9,2	3,6	9,0	8,2	Borduşani–Popină	Romania	Ch	
	tarsometatarsus						9,7	9,7	Tiszaszőlős–Domaháza	Hungary	N	
Larus argentatus	tibiotarsus	105,0							Maroslele–Pana	Hungary	N	
	tarsometatarsus	61,0							Maroslele–Pana	Hungary	N	
Grus grus	coracoideum					12,8		35,5	Vităneşti	Romania	Ch	
	carpometacarpus	121,0							Szolnok–Szanda	Hungary	N	
	carpometacarpus	125,0							Endrőd 39	Hungary	N	
	carpometacarpus			23,5					Vităneşti	Romania	Ch	
	phalanx anterior 1/II	ap. 47,0				13,6	7,1	11,9	Borduşani–Popină	Romania	Ch	
	phalanx anterior 1/II	53,4				15,5			Endrőd 39	Hungary	N	
	tibiotarsus					9,1	20,8	17,9	Coslogeni	Romania	N	
	tibiotarsus					10,5	23,0	21,7	Ecsegfalva 23	Hungary	N	
	tibiotarsus						20,5		Röszke–Lúdvár	Hungary	N	
	tibiotarsus						22,2	19,5	Vităneşti	Romania	Ch	
	tarsometatarsus			23,9	21,4	8,6			Căscioarele	Romania	Ch	
Anthropoides virgo	tibiotarsus						17,2	15,0	Vităneşti	Romania	Ch	
Tetrax tetrax	femur			15,0	10,0	5,8			Hârşova	Romania	Ch	
	tibiotarsus					4,9	9,0	9,1	Vităneşti	Romania	Ch	
Otis tarda	coracoideum	101,2	86,4			11,6	44,0	39,7	Vităneşti	Romania	Ch	male
	scapula		30,0			12,2			Vităneşti	Romania	Ch	male
	scapula		30,4						Vităneşti	Romania	Ch	male
	humerus			58,0					Endrőd 39	Hungary	N	male
	humerus						37,3		Borduşani–Popină	Romania	Ch	male
	ulna			20,0		8,8			Căscioarele	Romania	Ch	female
	ulna			25,5	30,0	12,2			Vităneşti	Romania	Ch	male
	radius			13,1	11,2				Vităneşti	Romania	Ch	male
	carpometacarpus	92,0							Endrőd 39	Hungary	N	female
	carpometacarpus	112,0							Endrőd 39	Hungary	N	male
	carpometacarpus			32,0					Endrőd 39	Hungary	N	male
	carpometacarpus			32,3					Vităneşti	Romania	Ch	male

Species	Skeletal Part	GL	SL	Bp	Dp	SC	Bd/Did	Dd	Site	Country	Age	Note
Otis tarda	carpometacarpus					13,4	13,5	11,0	Vităneşti	Romania	Ch	female
	carpometacarpus					17,4	16,6	12,7	Vităneşti	Romania	Ch	male
	carpometacarpus					13,6			Endrőd 39	Hungary	N	female
	carpometacarpus					17,0			Endrőd 39	Hungary	N	male
	phalanx anterior 1/II	50,2		12,4	9,7		13,8	7,3	Vităneşti	Romania	Ch	male
	phalanx anterior 1/II	52,4		12,5	10,0	14,6	12,8	7,5	Ecsegfalva 23	Hungary	N	male
	femur	125,0		34,0			32,0		Szolnok–Szanda	Hungary	N	male
	femur			34,5	23,2				Vităneşti	Romania	Ch	male
	femur						31,0		Endrőd 39	Hungary	N	male
	femur						31,5		Endrőd 39	Hungary	N	male
	tibiotarsus	220,0							Endrőd 39	Hungary	N	male
	tibiotarsus					9,3	16,7	17,5	Căscioarele	Romania	Ch	female
	tibiotarsus						17,0		Endrőd 39	Hungary	N	female
	tibiotarsus						17,6		Endrőd 39	Hungary	N	female
	tibiotarsus						24,0		Endrőd 39	Hungary	N	male
	tibiotarsus						20,6	22,9	Vităneşti	Romania	Ch	male
	tarsometatarsus			21,0					Endrőd 39	Hungary	N	male
Columba palumbus	coracoideum		40,7			4,6		12,0	Coslogeni	Romania	N	
	humerus			16,6					Ecsegfalva 23	Hungary	N	
	radius	54,2		4,9	4,9	2,5	5,6	3,4	Tiszaszőlős–Domaháza	Hungary	N	
	radius			5,0	4,1	2,3			Ecsegfalva 23	Hungary	N	
	radius					2,4	5,1	3,4	Ecsegfalva 23	Hungary	N	
	radius					2,4	5,7	3,6	Ecsegfalva 23	Hungary	N	
	radius					2,6			Ecsegfalva 23	Hungary	N	
	radius					2,6	5,9	3,4	Hârşova	Romania	Ch	
	radius					2,7	6,0	3,0	Hârşova	Romania	Ch	
	carpometacarpus	35,5		10,5		2,8	7,1	4,4	Ecsegfalva 23	Hungary	N	
	carpometacarpus	37,3				8,0	6,8	4,3	Ecsegfalva 23	Hungary	N	
	carpometacarpus	38,3		11,1		3,0	7,4		Ecsegfalva 23	Hungary	N	
	carpometacarpus			10,3		2,7			Ecsegfalva 23	Hungary	N	
	carpometacarpus			10,9					Ecsegfalva 23	Hungary	N	
	carpometacarpus			10,9					Ecsegfalva 23	Hungary	N	
	carpometacarpus			11,0		2,8			Ecsegfalva 23	Hungary	N	
	carpometacarpus						9,2	4,3	Ecsegfalva 23	Hungary	N	
	phalanx anterior 1/II	18,4				7,6			Ecsegfalva 23	Hungary	N	
	phalanx anterior 1/II	19,6		7,0	4,0	8,4	7,8		Ecsegfalva 23	Hungary	N	
	phalanx anterior 1/II	20,1		6,6	4,0	7,5	7,5	4,1	Ecsegfalva 23	Hungary	N	
	phalanx anterior 1/II	20,4				8,3	7,1	4,1	Ecsegfalva 23	Hungary	N	

147

Species	Skeletal Part	GL	SL	Bp	Dp	SC	Bd/Did	Dd	Site	Country	Age	Note
Columba palumbus	phalanx anterior 1/II	21,2			4,1	8,3	7,4	4,1	Ecsegfalva 23	Hungary	N	
	phalanx anterior 1/II			5,0					Ecsegfalva 23	Hungary	N	
	phalanx anterior 1/II			6,0	3,9				Ecsegfalva 23	Hungary	N	
	phalanx anterior 1/II			6,4	3,9				Ecsegfalva 23	Hungary	N	
	phalanx anterior 2/II			4,3					Ecsegfalva 23	Hungary	N	
	tibiotarsus						6,8		Röszke–Lúdvár	Hungary	N	
Bubo bubo	radius	177,0							Polgár–Csőszhalom	Hungary	N	
Strix aluco	humerus			15,3					Vitănești	Romania	Ch	
	ulna					4,0	7,5	6,3	Măgura–Buduiasca	Romania	N	
	phalanx anterior 1/II	18,9		4,6	3,9	6,5	5,1	3,8	Ecsegfalva 23	Hungary	N	
Asio flammeus	tarsometatarsus					4,1	10,0	7,1	Vitănești	Romania	Ch	
Coracias garrulus	coracoideum	ap. 30,0	28,4			2,2		8,1	Ecsegfalva 23	Hungary	N	
Upupa epops	humerus	31,9	14,1	8,5		3,1	7,8	4,1	Borduşani–Popină	Romania	Ch	
Dendrocopus major	ulna					2,3	4,5	3,6	Ecsegfalva 23	Hungary	N	
Alauda arvensis	ulna					1,9	3,5	2,5	Ecsegfalva 23	Hungary	N	
Riparia riparia	mandibula	17,4							Hârşova	Romania	Ch	
	sternum		18,0						Hârşova	Romania	Ch	
	humerus	12,3		5,3		1,7	3,8	2,4	Hârşova	Romania	Ch	
	pelvis	13,5	12,7						Hârşova	Romania	Ch	
Hirundo rustica	sternum		21,5						Hârşova	Romania	Ch	
	coracoideum	15,3	14,7			0,9		3,2	Hârşova	Romania	Ch	
	coracoideum	15,5	14,8			0,9		3,2	Hârşova	Romania	Ch	
	coracoideum	16,0	15,1			1,0		3,7	Hârşova	Romania	Ch	
	pelvis		13,5						Hârşova	Romania	Ch	
	humerus	15,3		5,8		1,9	4,5	2,8	Hârşova	Romania	Ch	
	radius	21,7		1,4	1,1	0,7	2,1	1,3	Hârşova	Romania	Ch	
	phalanx anterior 1/II	9,7		2,6	1,5	2,7			Hârşova	Romania	Ch	
	phalanx anterior 1/II	9,7		2,8	1,8	2,5			Hârşova	Romania	Ch	
Turdus pilaris	ulna	38,8		5,3	6,3	2,5	4,8	3,3	Vitănești	Romania	Ch	
Turdus viscivourus	tarsometatarsus	33,0		4,7	4,6	1,7	3,8	2,1	Ecsegfalva 23	Hungary	N	

Species	Skeletal Part	GL	SL	Bp	Dp	SC	Bd/Did	Dd	Site	Country	Age	Note
Garrulus glandarius	ulna					2,9	5,8	4,1	Ecsegfalva 23	Hungary	N	
	carpometacarpus			6,7		4,5			Hârşova	Romania	Ch	
Pica pica	humerus	48,8		14,2		4,5	11,3	6,2	Borduşani–Popină	Romania	Ch	
	humerus					ap. 4,2	10,5	5,9	Hârşova	Romania	Ch	
	ulna	52,8		7,6	7,9	3,5	6,9	5,0	Hârşova	Romania	Ch	
	ulna						6,9	4,9	Hârşova	Romania	Ch	
	radius			3,3	2,6	1,9			Hârşova	Romania	Ch	
	radius					1,8	4,0	2,7	Hârşova	Romania	Ch	
	carpometacarpus	31,0		7,8		5,4	7,4	2,8	Hârşova	Romania	Ch	
	carpometacarpus			7,3					Hârşova	Romania	Ch	
	tibiotarsus						5,7	5,5	Ecsegfalva 23	Hungary	N	
	tarsometatarsus	50,8		7,1	7,7	2,8	5,0	3,8	Borduşani–Popină	Romania	Ch	
Corvus frugilegus/C. corone	coracoideum	40,7				3,5			Hârşova	Romania	Ch	juvenile
	coracoideum	44,5	41,0			3,1	13,1	12,3	Borduşani–Popină	Romania	Ch	
	scapula		11,5			4,3			Borduşani–Popină	Romania	Ch	
	humerus	70,5		19,2		6,8			Măgura–Buduiasca	Romania	N	
	humerus			19,7		6,8			Borduşani–Popină	Romania	Ch	
	humerus			20,3		7,0			Borduşani–Popină	Romania	Ch	
	humerus					6,2	14,1	7,7	Hârşova	Romania	Ch	
	ulna	81,0		10,3		4,9	9,3	6,2	Hârşova	Romania	Ch	
	ulna	81,1		10,0	11,0	5,0	9,5	6,9	Borduşani–Popină	Romania	Ch	
	ulna	81,5		10,8	10,9	5,0	9,0	7,3	Borduşani–Popină	Romania	Ch	
	ulna	82,5		10,2		5,0	9,8	7,0	Hârşova	Romania	Ch	
	ulna			9,8		4,6			Hârşova	Romania	Ch	
	ulna			ap. 10,1	10,8	4,8			Borduşani–Popină	Romania	Ch	
	ulna			10,4	10,9	4,6			Borduşani–Popină	Romania	Ch	
	ulna			10,6		5,2	9,7	6,8	Borduşani–Popină	Romania	Ch	
	ulna					4,8	9,5	6,6	Borduşani–Popină	Romania	Ch	
	ulna					4,9	9,3	6,7	Isaccea	Romania	N	
	ulna					5,0	10,0	7,2	Borduşani–Popină	Romania	Ch	

Species	Skeletal Part	GL	SL	Bp	Dp	SC	Bd/Did	Dd	Site	Country	Age	Note
Corvus frugilegus/C. corone	ulna					5,2	9,6	7,0	Hârşova	Romania	Ch	
	radius					1,9	6,2	3,9	Hârşova	Romania	Ch	
	radius					2,4	6,3	4,0	Borduşani–Popină	Romania	Ch	
	carpometacarpus	45,2							Hârşova	Romania	Ch	
	carpometacarpus	49,9		11,5		8,1	11,0	4,4	Borduşani–Popină	Romania	Ch	
	carpometacarpus	50,3		12,0		7,4	9,6	4,5	Hârşova	Romania	Ch	
	carpometacarpus	52,4		11,5		8,4	11,5	4,6	Hârşova	Romania	Ch	
	femur	49,2	47,8	7,5	5,9	3,9	8,9	6,1	Borduşani–Popină	Romania	Ch	subadult
	femur	49,6	47,0	7,5	6,1	4,1	9,1	6,4	Borduşani–Popină	Romania	Ch	subadult
	tibiotarsus			10,8		4,5			Borduşani–Popină	Romania	Ch	
	tibiotarsus			13,2		3,9	8,5		Borduşani–Popină	Romania	Ch	
	tibiotarsus					3,9	8,9	7,4	Borduşani–Popină	Romania	Ch	
	tibiotarsus						7,9	7,4	Hârşova	Romania	Ch	
	tarsometatarsus					3,4		3,9	Hârşova	Romania	Ch	
Sturnus vulgaris	humerus	28,8		9,1		2,9	7,4	3,5	Ecsegfalva 23	Hungary	N	
	humerus			8,2		2,5		3,2	Ecsegfalva 23	Hungary	N	
	humerus			8,8		2,8			Ecsegfalva 23	Hungary	N	
	humerus						6,9	3,4	Ecsegfalva 23	Hungary	N	
	ulna					2,0	4,0	2,9	Ecsegfalva 23	Hungary	N	
	ulna					2,1	4,1	2,8	Ecsegfalva 23	Hungary	N	
Passer domesticus	humerus	18,8		6,0		1,8	4,9	2,3	Ecsegfalva 23	Hungary	N	
	humerus			6,1		1,7			Ecsegfalva 23	Hungary	N	

ARCHAEOLINGUA

Edited by
ERZSÉBET JEREM and WOLFGANG MEID

Main Series

1. **Cultural and Landscape Changes in South-East Hungary. I: Reports on the Gyomaendrőd Project.** Edited by Sándor Bökönyi. 1992. 384 pp. € 36.-. ISBN 963 7391 60 6.

2. Stefan Schumacher: **Die rätischen Inschriften. Geschichte und heutiger Stand der Forschung.** 1992. 2. vermehrte Auflage 2004. 375 pp. € 62.-. ISBN 963 8046 53 8.

5. **Cultural and Landscape Changes in South-East Hungary. II.** Edited by Sándor Bökönyi. 1996. 453 pp. € 36.-. ISBN 963 8046 04 X.

7. **Die Osthallstattkultur. Akten des Internationalen Symposiums, Sopron, 10. – 14. Mai 1994.** Herausgegeben von Erzsébet Jerem und Andreas Lippert. 1996. 588 pp. € 88.-. ISBN 963 8046 10 4.

8. **Man and the Animal World. Studies in Archaeozoology, Archaeology, Anthropology and Palaeolinguistics in memoriam Sándor Bökönyi**. Edited by Peter Anreiter, László Bartosiewicz, Erzsébet Jerem and Wolfgang Meid. 1998. 720 pp. € 92.-. ISBN 963 8046 15 5.

9. **Archaeology of the Bronze and Iron Age – Environmental Archaeology, Experimental Archaeology, Archaeological Parks. Proceedings of the International Archaeological Conference, Százhalombatta, 3–7 October, 1996.** Edited by Erzsébet Jerem and Ildikó Poroszlai. 1999. 488 pp. € 68.-. ISBN 963 8046 25 2.

11. **From the Mesolithic to the Neolithic. Proceedings of the International Archaeological Conference held in the Damjanich Museum of Szolnok, September 22–27, 1996.** Edited by Róbert Kertész and János Makkay. 2001. 461 pp. € 72.-. ISBN 963 8046 35 X.

12. Garrett Olmsted: **Celtic Art in Transition during the First Century BC. An Examination of the Creations of Mint Masters and Metal Smiths, and an Analysis of Stylistic Development during the Phase between La Tène and Provincial Roman.** 2001. 340 pp., with 142 plates. € 72.-. ISBN 963 8046 37 6.

13. **The Archaeology of Cult and Religion.** Edited by Peter F. Biehl and François Bertemes with Harald Meller. 2001. 288 pp. € 68.-. ISBN 963 8046 38 4.

15. **Morgenrot der Kulturen. Frühe Etappen der Menschheitsgeschichte in Mittel- und Südosteuropa. Festschrift für Nándor Kalicz zum 75. Geburtstag.** Herausgegeben von Erzsébet Jerem und Pál Raczky. 2003. 570 pp. € 78.-. ISBN 963 8046 46 5.
16. **The Geohistory of Bátorliget Marshland.** Edited by Pál Sümegi and Sándor Gulyás. 2004. 360 pp. € 66.-. ISBN 963 8046 47 3.
17. **Nord-Süd, Ost-West. Kontakte während der Eisenzeit in Europa. Akten der Internationalen Tagungen der AG Eisenzeit in Hamburg und Sopron 2002.** Herausgegeben von Erzsébet Jerem, Martin Schönfelder und Günther Wieland. 2006. ca. 320 pp. € 84.-. ISBN 963 8046 57 0.
18. Raimund Karl: **Altkeltische Sozialstrukturen.** 2006. 609 pp. € 78.-. ISBN 963 8046 69 4.
19. Martin Hannes Graf: **Schaf und Ziege im frühgeschichtlichen Mitteleuropa. Sprach- und kulturgeschichtliche Studien.** 2006. 320 pp. € 60.-. ISBN 963 8046 70 8.
20. **Anthropology of the Indo-European World and Material Culture. Proceedings of the 5th International Colloquium of Anthropology of the Indo-European World and Comparative Mythology.** Edited by Marco V. García Quintela, Francisco J. González García and Felipe Criado Boado. 2006. 368 pp. € 64.-. ISBN 963 8046 72 4.

Series Minor

4. Ferenc Gyulai: **Environment and Agriculture in Bronze Age Hungary.** 1993. 59 pp. € 18.-. ISBN 963 7391 66 5.
6. Marija Gimbutas: **Das Ende Alteuropas. Der Einfall von Steppennomaden aus Südrußland und die Indogermanisierung Mitteleuropas.** 1994. 2. Aufl. 2000. 135 pp. € 32.-. ISBN 963 8046 09 0.
7. Eszter Bánffy: **Cult Objects of the Neolithic Lengyel Culture. Connections and Interpretation.** 1997. 131 pp. € 26.-. ISBN 963 8046 16 3.
10. Nándor Kalicz: **Figürliche Kunst und bemalte Keramik aus dem Neolithikum Westungarns.** 1998. 156 pp. € 30.-. ISBN 963 8046 19 8.
11. **Transhumant Pastoralism in Southern Europe. Recent Perspectives from Archaeology, History and Ethnology.** Edited by Haskel J. Greenfield and László Bartosiewicz. 1999. 245 pp. € 36.-. ISBN 963 8046 11 2.
12. Francisco Marco Simón: **Die Religion im keltischen Hispanien.** 1998. 168 pp. € 32.-. ISBN 963 8046 24 4.
13. Peter Raulwing: **Horses, Chariots and Indo-Europeans. Problems of Chariotry Research from the Viewpoint of Indo-European Linguistics.** 2000. 210 pp. € 36.-. ISBN 963 8046 26 0.

14. John Chapman: **Tension at Funerals – Micro-Tradition Analysis in Later Hungarian Prehistory.** 2000. 184 pp. € 32.-. ISBN 963 8046 29 5.
15. Eszter Bánffy: **A Unique Prehistoric Figurine of the Near East.** 2001. 106 pp. € 24.-. ISBN 963 8046 36 8.
17. Paul Gaechter: **Die Gedächtniskultur in Irland.** 2003. 116 pp. € 20.-. ISBN 963 8046 45 7.
18. **The Geoarchaeology of River Valleys.** Edited by Halina Dobrzańska, Erzsébet Jerem and Tomasz Kalicki. 2004. 214 pp. € 38.-. ISBN 963 8046 48 1.
19. Karin Stüber: **Schmied und Frau. Studien zur gallischen Epigraphik und Onomastik.** 2004. 125 pp. € 24.-. ISBN 963 8046 55 4.
21. **The Archaeology of Cult and Death. Proceedings of the Session "The Archaeology of Cult and Death" Organized for the 9th Annual Meeting of the European Association of Archaeologists, 11th September 2003, St. Petersburg, Russia.** Edited by Mercourios Georgiadis and Chrysanthi Gallou. 2006. 194 pp. € 32.-. ISBN 963 8046 67 8.
22. **Landscape Ideologies.** Edited by Thomas Meier. 2006. 260 pp. € 34.-. ISBN 963 8046 71 6.
23. **The Archaeology of Fire. Understanding Fire as Material Culture.** Edited by Dragos Gheorghiu and George Nash. 2007. 261 pp. € 34.-. ISBN 978-963-8046-79-6.
24. Erika Gál: **Fowling in Lowlands. Neolithic and Chalcolithic Bird Exploitation in South-East Romania and the Great Hungarian Plain.** 2007. 149 pp. € 28.-. ISBN 978-963-8046-85-7.
25. Anthony Harding: **Warriors and Weapons in Bronze Age Europe.** 2007. 224 pp. € 36.-. ISBN 978-963-8046-86-4.

Praehistoria

1. **Praehistoria. International prehistory journal of the University of Miskolc.** Edited by Árpád Ringer, Zsolt Mester and Erzsébet Jerem. **Volume 1, 2000.** 188 pp. € 32.-. **Volume 2, 2001.** 201 pp. € 34.-. **Volume 3, 2002.** 338 pp. € 40.-. **Volume 4–5, 2003–2004.** 247 pp. € 35.-. **Volume 6, 2005.** 130 pp. € 30.-. HU ISSN 1586 7811.

Please address orders to:
ARCHAEOLINGUA
H-1250 Budapest, Pf. 41.
Fax: (+361) 3758939
e-mail: kovacsr@archaeolingua.hu   http://www.archaeolingua.hu/